mama

Through Spiritual Eyes

The Journey From Within And Beyond

By Carole Marlene Sletta

Foreword And Compilation By
Cheryl Long Riffle, RSc.P

AmErica House
Baltimore

First printing

ISBN: 1-59129-256-5
PUBLISHED BY AMERICA HOUSE BOOK PUBLISHERS
www.publishamerica.com
Baltimore

Printed in the United States of America

Acknowledgments

To my husband Ron, for always being there with his love and strength, especially when I needed him the most. To my children: Kimberely, Teresa, Stephen, Heather, Michael; and my grandchildren: Christopher, Ashley, Jacob, Joshua, Madeline, Nadika and Samantha, for their constant source of love and joy.

To Brooke; for reopening the door to the other side allowing me to consider and know for myself that angels do in fact exist; and to realize that they are there to help guide us if we just choose to listen.

To my incredible friends who inspired me to put Cameron and Rachelle's words into book form. To Nancy for introducing and awakening me to the gift of channeling. To Joni Heyman and Lizzy Shannon for their suggestions and encouragement. Thanks also to Cheryl for her expertise and endless hours of labor in transforming *Through Spiritual Eyes* into perfect manuscript form, and for our priceless friendship that has grown from this!

To my therapists who encouraged me with love and caring compassion; they were able to pull me out of my deepest despair and show me I was precious when I felt so worthless. The acquired belief in myself has become my most priceless gift.

Table of Contents

"What lies behind us and what lies before us are small matters compared to what lies within us."
Ralph Waldo Emerson

Foreword

Carole Sletta has been an intuitive since childhood but it was only as an adult that she came to understand her gift. *Through Spiritual Eyes* begins with her awakening and emerging into the gifted intuitive she was always meant to be. Once aware, she channels two highly evolved angelic beings. The first is Cameron, her trusted guide who later introduces her to Rachelle, a spirit of such gentleness and scope of being that we must breathe large to encompass who she is. Carole, who shares this journey and her insights along the way, is the soul of truth, refreshing at any time, but especially appreciated today.

It is my role to be Watson to Sherlock. Carole is an extremely clear channel, equal in her own way as an expert Sherlock. I am the one who listens, speaks to Cameron and Rachelle and compiles this remarkable odyssey.

Cameron was originally recorded on tape then carefully transcribed word for word by Carole. At that time I entered the picture to put the material into book form. Everything has a purpose, and it was different than I thought. I found myself hesitating to make even a small correction in anything from Cameron or Rachelle. Cameron comes through with a strong East Indian accent and his English often needed some rearranging for readability. Rachelle's voice is quiet, soft and feels like a wrap-around whisper. Her clear and precise words required little adjusting. In order to edit their material for clarity I had to gain confidence to edit angelic beings.

At first, I would speak to Carole about a change or correction and she would speak to Cameron who would usually say, "Fine, go ahead." He encouraged me to continue my editing without always going through Carole. This forced me to ask and listen to them myself. My intuitive ability grew and soon I was able to communicate with either of these spirits directly and receive a response. In time I became confident and guided and knew this was all part of the grand design of our work together. They have come to feel like trusted friends and teachers.

These wise beings honor and value every soul. They touched Carole and me, not only to bring this book to you; but to assist us on our journey of light. They taught us to trust ourselves, find our inner wisdom and expand our abilities first, so that we could confidently bring this material to others. I know there is a purpose within this book for everyone it touches.

Let me describe a typical session with Rachelle so that you can better visualize the process of obtaining this material. Carole and I meet in a quiet, comfortable room. We become still and I invite Rachelle to come in and speak with me. Upon that invitation a remarkable transformation takes place. Carole, who is often just a bit anxious before channeling Rachelle, becomes visibly calm, her body relaxes, she sits erectly, her hands compose together as if she were entering into meditation and a small smile comes to her lips. It is then that Rachelle greets me. She is always soft, gracious, gentle, and speaks in a voice just above a whisper.

Sometimes there is a question or two that Carole and I have from a previous session and I ask them at that time. Next, I tell her that we are ready for another chapter. There is a small pause, as if she is conferring, and indeed, she does say there are many spirits and she is the voice, then she suggests a chapter title and I, like the good Watson, am ready to take notes. But being an updated Watson, I type in what Rachelle says on my trusty Macintosh laptop computer.

Most of the time I can keep up with what she says, as she knows, I am typing; and she seems to try and pace herself to my needs. Rachelle is a very thoughtful presence. However, if she does get ahead of me I leave a space and pick it up later from the tape recording that we make of each session. At the close of her communication, she says goodbye and Carole opens her eyes. Carole immediately asks me to read her Rachelle's words. After that, we talk about the subjects.

Later I go over my typing and make any obvious corrections, usually typos or capitals. Since I am typing quickly I often leave these out so that I can stay up with her. An additional bit of editing needed is the addition of punctuation, for Rachelle, like Cameron, gives us the spoken word and, unlike Victor Borge's famous routine, does not give any punctuation or paragraph breaks.

I record each session with Rachelle as faithfully as did Watson but without his embellishments. I also listen to what she says and note any questions I have on the subjects. Both Cameron and Rachelle always answer our questions that are incorporated, when needed, into a chapter to clarify a subject. Finally, both of us re-read the chapters in depth for understanding and add any additional questions.

Cameron and Rachelle often awaken new thoughts or ways of looking at life that greatly expand our vision. It is our hope that you find this book as valuable, enlightening and applicable to your life as it has been to ours, for unlike Watson's recordings of fiction, this book is most wonderfully and remarkably non-fiction.

Cheryl Long Riffle, Rsc.P

Prologue

My search for the light began with much darkness. I believe I asked for parents to teach me many difficult lessons. The main one being self-love. They did this in such a way that from infancy on I was searching for approval.

Because I was not always nurtured at home and some of my emotional needs were not met, I relied primarily on myself. I grew up in nice homes and desirable neighborhoods with an abundance of material possessions. Everything appeared perfect to an onlooker. However, the most important needs that I sought, to feel loved and special, were lacking. Later I understood that my parents could not teach confidence and self-love to a child when they had none themselves.

The Catholic Church was very important to our family so, of course, I was reared accordingly. I sometimes felt comfort in being able to confide to a special nun about home secrets, but by the look on her face I discovered these were things that should stay that way— secret! The effect of my telling family happenings sometimes brought consequences at home so I decided it best to remain silent. I remember my father saying I was stupid and that people would not and did not believe me. I lived in a hidden world of family secrets. When I felt lonely I would listen to the constant low chatter I heard within or watch the light blue and white see-through people all around me, becoming mesmerized by their comforting murmurs.

As a child, I listened and observed people as they answered questions. I thought it was a confusing and funny type of game when

I saw their hearts and the see-through people express a different response. Somehow the answers from their hearts and the see-throughs always felt right. I began to play along wanting to answer the questions too. I did this without anyone knowing and kept the answers to myself. The fun diminished as I realized their hearts, the see-through people, and I always seemed to come up with the same answers. I accepted this everyday seeing, hearing and playing with those I called the see-through people as a normal way of life. It was not until I became an adult that I realized everyone did not hear, see and feel into the physic realm as I did.

My search for self has spanned over half a century. At one point I concluded that everything that was wrong in my life could be cured if I just lost that extra twenty pounds. With that thought as my catalyst, I started on a relentless search for a miracle cure through the latest diet, new weight-loss gimmick, or magic pill. This consumed much of my time. It worked for a while but somehow the weight always became a part of me again.

Finally I found my way to a loving therapist with the intention of working on my weight issue. When asked about my life, I discovered I had no deep feelings about it but I felt rather numb. I soon learned that the extra weight was my cover-up for other unresolved issues. The safety I felt with my primary counselor allowed me to continue without fear. Far into my healing two more gifted people also helped me. The therapists let me find my own truth while giving me love and strength as I discovered all the hidden parts of myself. Uncovering my childhood abuse was the hardest thing I have ever done! It was also the best gift I have given myself.

Self-discovery was amazing. Now I can have feelings, thoughts, and opinions. I can laugh, cry, and be happy, sad, or even mad—a big one to give myself permission to do—and it's okay. I learned forgiveness. I like myself. I'm not stupid. What a revelation! I can do anything I choose, so many choices. The sky's the limit. Finally my life seemed rich and full, but actually I had barely begun to awaken.

Carole

Cameron

Cameron tells us he lived his last earthly life in India, over two hundred years ago, where he died at the age of thirty-two. He comes as a male-female entity with the culmination of knowledge from all his lives. Cameron says his wisdom in this book is not his alone but rather from a collection of many conferring spirits. Often he states "we" to acknowledge this spiritual group consciousness.

We asked him how the group answers worked. He explained, "When a question is asked it is not just directed to me, it is directed to anyone in the spirit world who has their 'blinders' off. So what I take in is the feel of the answer from those spirits, much like telepathic communication; from this I conclude what your answer would be. It is as if we are in unison, we feel all your questions; it is a deep knowing of the answer that guides us. We do not claim to be any smarter than you, but with our broadened vision we are able to see ahead on your chosen path. It is just that humans have to experience a situation in order to see ahead, they need a past to make a judgment, but we see future and past. It is like your car is working on one spark plug while on earth. Here we have all the spark plugs hooked up, so it is not a better vehicle but one that has all the parts working together."

When asked why he communicated with us he replied, "I am an observer to the ones I love most. My heart's desire is for earth to be a place of peace for all of you. In many of my lives I have not been at peace, while in some I have. Through many lifetimes I know the difficulty you experience on earth. I wish I could show you how easy being on earth can be. It's one of the most beautiful events that can happen.

"Safety on earth is a huge concern to many. Security is often felt when you are confined. Here the word boundary is a non-word. So allow me to be your eyes, just for now, perhaps I can help. I am the same as you, not different. I am able to draw on my earth time to understand. When you are here, you are everything. However, on earth one selects a box to be in and takes a name, such as Cameron, or another. Now I prefer to spend all of my time in observation of the ones I love, but oh the heartache I see. I feel that I can best help with the expanded view from here."

When Cameron is present his energy is often felt by others in the room. Many sense he is East Indian; some say they can "see" he is of slight build, has dark skin and very dark eyes. A few have shared with Carole that when she is channeling him they can see his body transformed over hers. They say he sits cross-legged in her lap and his expressive dark eyes can be seen on her closed eyelids. They say his loving energy feels comforting to them.

All are in agreement that he is like an old trusted friend, someone you can tell anything to without judgment. Cameron is a reliable guide that can help anyone in getting down to the core of their question or problem and assist them in uncovering their own truth. He has only unconditional love and the highest respect for all of us on earth.

We have found Cameron to be a most loving, gentle, kind, and extremely humble spiritual presence. (In fact, it was difficult to get him to speak about himself.) He does not proclaim to have our answers but assures each of us that they are indeed within us. In this book he guides us in reclaiming our own untapped wisdom.

PART ONE

Awakening

CHAPTER 1

The Dawn of Awareness

Carole

On a beautiful, warm October day in 1993 while watching my son's soccer game, I became aware of a young woman trying to get my attention. Her warm smile felt like an invitation to meet. While chatting she introduced herself as Nancy. We found that our sons were on the same newly formed team.

Nancy told me she felt the strong awareness of spiritual beings around me. She offered guidance to assist me in communicating with them if I was interested. I had not given spirits much thought in my adult years to know what to think about this, but I was a bit intrigued. Curiosity took over and we exchanged phone numbers.

Two weeks later Nancy guided me in a relaxing visualization. While doing this I saw a man standing near a brook and felt he wanted to speak. I was waiting to hear his words when within an instant I found his words coming out of my mouth and in a masculine voice! This was very embarrassing and felt awkward. I had no idea what was going on but she explained that I was channeling. This was a new word for me and I really did not understand its full meaning. But I wanted to know how I was able to hear his words, see detailed pictures, feel the emotions related to them, and have a constant awareness of my surroundings, all at the same time! This began my re-acquaintance to my spirit guides and began a new awakening to the possibilities they offered.

After years of channeling many different angelic beings I felt my search for purpose and self begin to emerge as I listened and asked questions of one particular spirit named Cameron. He has a wonderful peace about him, continually offering me new ways to view experiences all while stretching my understanding with love. I felt in alignment with Cameron and he became my chosen guide.

Within two years of choosing Cameron as my guide he introduced me to Rachelle. She felt like a soft whispering force of continuing knowledge and remembrance for me. Cameron would introduce me to a thought, as if setting down a foundation, and then Rachelle would lovingly help me expand upon that thought for my increased awareness. Together I found them to be the perfect teachers of the deep inner growth I had been craving for so long.

Due to this, I wanted to share Cameron and Rachelle's insights in *Through Spiritual Eyes*. These gentle spirits have remained constant in their love and expansive wisdom while guiding others and myself on our journey of life. This book shares their ideas and teachings. May you also be touched by the light of their love and wisdom.

"Everyone is special, like part of a kaleidoscope."
Cameron

CHAPTER 2

Embracing Your Beauty

Cameron

Our purpose in this book is to help you find your beauty and divinity. We wish to assist in uncovering these qualities in each of you. There are many ways to do this.

We all start out as a wonderful soul seed of light that we must nurture in order to grow. Everyone's essence is love and beauty but often the displeasures in your world create layers of darkness that wrap around this beautiful soul light. Everyone is special, like part of a kaleidoscope. You are all precious and must find your own beauty; it is there, underneath the layers. These layers are made up of the consequences and experiences that happen to you. Because you have had many troubling times in your life your inner light becomes covered much like a cocoon.

Often negative things happen to people. Positive things happen too, but frequently most of you don't feel worthy of this goodness. Through many years of unpleasant happenings the light of your soul becomes covered. As an adult you may think: Who am I? What is this all about? What am I here for? Many people then begin the huge job of uncovering their inner light.

Your perfect soul seed is seeking light. It is difficult to seek when that seed is tightly bound in a cocoon. The Divine Light is drawing close to everyone all the time. However, you cannot feel this draw if your soul is cocooned in darkness. Remember we are all spirits of light.

Your soul in the cocoon state would be like a very tightly closed hand-held fan. For a moment, visualize that fan in your heart area. If you were to allow the fan in your heart area to open, you would be able to receive guidance for your highest good. When you learn to keep the fan open at all times, your guidance is whole, pure, perfect and beautiful. Let us explain how to do this.

It is possible to ask yourself a question and receive an answer for your highest good by the "fan" method. Begin by visualizing a hand-held fan that will expand and close. See it in your heart area. Now picture it closed. Then ask a simple question where the answer would obviously be a "no." When the fan remains tightly closed, this means "no," and may give you a feeling of tightness in your heart-chest area.

Next, ask a simple question where the answer is obviously "yes." When the fan opens wide in response to your question, this means a "yes" answer. You may also feel an expansion or freeing in your heart-chest area, this is another way it says "yes."

Remember to check in with your heart and ask the questions before acting upon a decision. Practice this for several weeks, with simple questions, to get the feel of the answers. Your mind may want to override the answer from your heart but take a small risk and follow your yes or no answers. As you continue to do this freeing exercise you will feel your answers more surely and quickly. By following your open yes fan, you will be open to the light of truth. This can be your guiding instrument for life. When you learn to feel the fan expansion and fan closing, you will have found a way to navigate life. You will also realize your life can be interesting, beautiful, and totally freeing.

You may wonder why you can get your answers from this method. It is just a way of connecting with the truth of yourself, your inner wisdom and through this, connecting to the Divine Essence. For we are all connected, we are all connected to the Creator therefore we are all Oneself.

The love and wisdom of the Creator can freely come to you

through an open fan. Your own pure truth is also received this way. Listen to your inner wisdom. If you visualize or feel a closed fan, stop and do not go further with that idea or thought, for that is not where the light is. If you visualize or feel an open fan, go forward, for you now are stepping onto your guided path of light.

Carole

Channeling Cameron started at a time when I needed a big dose of self-love and trust. His name for me is "this one." I always thought that was endearing. But it took me well over a year to trust that I was not somehow making his voice up.

How could this masculine and foreign sounding voice be coming out of my mouth? As Cameron talked to my friends, I saw everything in pictures. It seemed like I was viewing a vivid color movie. Sometimes the scenes would backtrack to past lives or move forward thirty or forty years. At other times I could see a person passing from earth. Years would skip by in a millisecond, but it all made sense and didn't seem fast at the time. I was also surprised to feel the emotions of the person I was channeling for or any others I was viewing in a scene. I could feel their hurt, sadness, fear, and could also feel their joy, happiness or peace. This all occurred at once. What was going on? Was I crazy? Why was this happening to me?

My parents, siblings and I drew apart when I was undergoing therapy even though I thought we had always been a close family. My sister and I tried to talk a few times on the phone, but fumbling for the proper words was too uncomfortable. We had clearly chosen different paths. Silence was the best my parents and brother could offer me through the many struggles with my childhood memories. That hurt could not have cut any deeper. On many occasions the thought of suicide sounded all too welcome and seemed the only way out of my private hell. What stopped me was the feeling that somehow my parents would "get me" when they died.

When the pain became too unbearable, I decided to legally change my first and middle names so that I could try to disassociate from the hurt little Carole had endured. With the name Karmen Marie I found new strength. As I moved deeper into my pain and through my healing, I was able to go back to the courts months later and reclaim my old name. That felt very empowering!

My husband and children were my pillars of strength and sanity throughout my therapy. I still felt isolated and longed for my mother, father, and siblings, though, to complete my family. Cameron came at a time when I was wavering. I hoped it might be possible to make peace with my family. I could go back, face my family, apologize for telling my truth, and pretend everything was okay. I often thought of this and each time I did it caused me great dismay and thrust me into darkness. My thinking at the time was that at least this way I might be able to get my family back. However, I was no longer willing to pretend that everything was okay when it was not. A path of light was calling to me and the way seemed well defined. Could I trust it? Could I trust my judgment? Was I making this all up? I put my trust in Cameron. What could I lose at this point?

I tried to lead my life for the next year based on the fan expansion in my chest. In the beginning I had to remain quiet to visualize the fan. But after a few weeks I could feel whether it was open or closed. If it felt partly closed, I would go deeper with my questions until total expansion or closure was felt.

Just as I was starting this book, my father died. Because of all my surfacing memories and unfolding discoveries I had not seen nor talked to him in over two years. Days after his passing I was shocked to hear his voice state, "You are the strong one. I am weak." Earth binds us so tightly sometimes that the truth cannot be spoken. With his passing over he became free and my father's words in spirit freed me as well. I know now the path of light via the fan holds only truth for me. Life is so peaceful and freeing when I just listen to my inner voice and feel the expansion. I now trust that truth and goodness will always follow.

"Truth is found when you trust your heart for your guidance."
Cameron

CHAPTER 3

Your Path of Truth

Cameron

Truth tends to wear many masks. People often mask the truth by saying, "Oh, believe me, I'm telling the truth," when in fact, it frequently is a denial of truth. So do be cautious when you listen to others. While talking to others or yourself monitoring your truth might also be appropriate.

The path of truth is really your ticket to the light. When you are in a fan expansion, you will find that only truth can be spoken; not truth with masks, *pure* truth. The fan can be your constant guidance. If you keep your fan open, your life can remain very simple and uncomplicated. When truth comes with many masks on it, life gets very complicated and unsettled.

If you could remain with your fan open, truth will come to you. People do not like to hover around others when *only* truth is spoken. We see people remain in an untruthful state when they do not feel good about themselves. This is as far as you can possibly be away from self. It is quite necessary for your wholeness to be one with God.

When we use the word "God," that is our chosen word. You may wish for other words. Please use "Being," "Light" or anything that is higher to self that you can rely on. Anything that you can really depend on that has the strength of love, but not power over you. If we use the word "God" we do not want anyone to feel uncomfortable.

This word is comfortable for this one (Carole) who I am speaking through. Use any word that brings you comfort.

The path of light can serve you for an eternity; it can serve everyone. You can go any place you want with this. You could become the wealthiest person in the world, but true wealth is really being filled with light. Learn to trust yourself, trust the fan, and trust the light. This takes a lot of energy and a lot of self-love.

To be able to feel the expansion in your chest always feels so good and wonderful. The problem on earth seems to be in trusting. People often say, "Well, my head does not think that, so how can it be truth?" Truth is found when you trust your heart for guidance.

Heads are wonderful but often can be an escape avenue for people when they really do not want to speak the truth. People can get into their heads and mull things over many times until it comes out and sounds correct to them, but it is actually distorted. If guidance does not come from your heart and soul, it is usually not what you are seeking. If you could continue to trust your feelings and the expansion in your chest, nothing but truth would come to you. Also know that consequences can become larger when you get into your head too much. It is possible to ignore the expanded feeling in your heart-soul area, but why would you want to do so?

Remember that you started out as a beautiful little seed, however through the years many earthly layers of events were building up, creating a binding of your soul. These layers are the consequences and experiences that happen to you. When too many layers bind you it is difficult to see and feel the light.

It's sad for us to see how many people are wounded; some by other people while many others may wound themselves. How could this happen? How could you wound yourself? The answer is: when you are in a state of comparing yourself to others and see yourself as less than they are, your soul binds tighter. Rejoice in who you are.

Compare yourself to no one! Sometimes on earth you are your own harshest critic. Often people wound others when their hurt is intense and they think, "I must pass this hurt on to someone else; it will be less on me."

To find your source of light, could you step down from your head and hover in the soul area? Just try and see how that would feel. See if the little tiny voice that you hear way down deep in your heart-soul area could be correct. Would it be worth giving credence to that little voice and see where it takes you? Try this a couple of times when the consequences wouldn't be big and see what happens. See what the outcome is, even though your head may completely flip it over by saying, "That is not true; it is nonsense." Trying this just a few times could be your assurance that this is truth. Without following your heart-soul area, nothing of importance can be accomplished. This is one of the most important teachings.

Money is very important on earth. It is not important to the soul. The soul only wishes for goodness. If you put all your energies into the knowledge that you have stored in your heart-soul area your head will follow. Your soul will be in total agreement that this is the truth. This takes a risk to do and is uncommon for most people. What you are all striving for is the light, but often you cannot see this because you are bound so tightly. We believe that when you follow your heart's wisdom many great things will come. Your life will be full. It is important to follow your paths; goodness will come to you when you do.

Carole

Cameron made a statement that really gave me an unsettled feeling. He said, "People do not like to hover around others when *only* truth is spoken." I felt sure this needed to be edited out; he must have gotten it mixed up. However, a decision was made long ago, that none of Cameron's concepts would be eliminated, so his statement stayed in, but his words still gnawed at me. I was truthful, I was sure of that, and I liked to be around those who spoke truth, so what did he mean? I can only apply this to my own life. I know that if people really shared what was always on their mind, their opinions or feelings, speaking only their truth, it would cause a lot of stirring. I get an uncomfortable feeling just thinking about it. A comfort buffer would seem necessary.

I spoke my truth to my parents and siblings and immediately became detached from them. It was as if I was on the outside looking in. I did not buffer my truth for them. My truth scared my family away. Cameron was right!

Many times going back and smoothing things over with my parents and siblings seemed the only way. Not being able to visit or talk to them affected so many parts of my life, especially during the holidays. Often I would go through the process of rejoining them in my mind, but each time I did the fan in my chest stayed so tightly closed that I ached.

I decided to continue to trust, and trust I did. Following my expanded fan led me to some of the most beautiful souls. I can hardly believe the goodness that has come to me this way through new-found friends, and old friendships, which have been strengthened. I feel so blessed as my second family now surrounds me in light.

"Each person has their own power inside of them."
Cameron

CHAPTER 4

Masking Truth

Cameron

Truth can hide behind many different masks so use caution. Little children believe their mothers and fathers stand for truth. Unfortunately, there are many parents that are not truthful. Truth may be hidden, by a mother wearing a mother mask, and father wearing a father mask. For instance, a father might hide behind his mask of power and position in the family. A mother might hide behind her mask of care taking, nurturing and busyness. When a small child believes that their parents only speak truth they become blinded to truth, by their parents' masks.

This happens more often than you might think. Many children are wounded this way. They reason, "I will trust them because they are my parents." Children often go back to parents who have offended them many times. They feel secure in this familiar cycle, which is understandable.

It is necessary to bring about a greater awareness of childhood trauma. As adults become more aware their knowledge of this will pass on to the children. Adults need to realize that sometimes even their own mothers and fathers, though held sacred to them, could have been harmful to them. The same can sometimes be true of churches where people can also hide behind their masks. If something *seems* truthful to you, but does not feel right in the heart-soul area, examine it further.

Distinguished credentials or a great amount of wealth does not guarantee that truth will be spoken. They can often be a cover up. We do not like to lump everyone together. There certainly *are* truthful people in powerful positions. Just be cautious, be very, very cautious on what you accept as truth.

Many professions often carry a lot of power on earth. Individuals with great power are often scared. They started out as a lovely seed, as we all did, but their experiences and consequences created their heart and soul to become tightly bound. Due to that they had to get into their head. They became very brilliant in the mind, but somehow the heart and soul got lost. It is tightly bound behind so much of their life experiences. Frequently we see those with a lot of power misuse it so much because they are very wounded, not always, but often.

Our caution to you is to avoid putting those with power on a pedestal. Do not believe everything they say. Somehow they think they must wound others to make themselves feel better. They can wound others in so many ways. This only brings them sadness and so they reach for more power, which creates a vicious circle. Our only purpose in telling you this is to emphasize that "caution" is a necessary word here. If you follow your heart you would not be tricked by the pedestal position.

We find those with great power would really like to strive for the light but often don't know how. Their power has gotten so large that it creates many walls that are hard to break down. Power and money have become all important to them. This brings us great sorrow. On earth some think power means truth. Certainly everyone in a powerful position is not untruthful. Just be more aware about believing what people say. Sometimes people get so awed by another's power that they do not even try to look within that person; they just want to see what their shell represents to them.

People with power and money can be rude to others. They may even slough people off and surprisingly the one being ignored can say, "Well, that's okay, they have a lot of money." That is so sad, especially for the one doing the hurting. It would be wonderful if we could touch some of these people in powerful positions. That higher power is in their mind and in the minds of others, but the truth is that everyone is absolutely the same.

We all start out as the same beautiful seed of light. Only experiences push some onto a pedestal very, very fast. Often they don't even know what hit them and they're on this pedestal and saying, "What happened? I don't know how I got here; I don't have all the answers like others think I do. What can I do?" So they often put a big shield tightly around them to keep people away. Sometimes they treat others unkindly. We would like to bless them because they have asked for a very hard lesson in order to learn much.

Power often scares people. We see people with extreme power frequently have to have guards to keep others away from them. That is unfortunate. Their soul is searching for so much more. But how do they start to unravel? It's often too big a job and too much face for them to lose.

It would please us to be able to reach everyone. In our eyes you are all exactly the same, all are perfect, each person has their own power inside of them. We would hope that those reading this book could find their own power. Only then will everyone be on the same level, no one will appear higher than anyone else.

The next time you watch a star on stage, screen or television, just know that they have been given a fake power without even knowing it. Perhaps you can think to yourself, "This is not only someone famous, this is also a beautiful soul." Know that you are both the same and heading for the same path of light. To give people special reverence does not empower their soul. Their soul does not want to be treated differently. If anyone ever thinks they deserve to be treated very highly, that is coming from their mind. Do a kindness, next time treat them as you wish to be treated. You might then get a flicker of light from within their beautiful soul.

We want to bless all on earth who are in high positions or have a famous or powerful name. They have asked for a very difficult task and would like for their experience on earth to teach them a great deal. Please, next time you are in a situation where you are around them remember to bless these "bigger than life" people on their path.

Carole

This chapter's title, "Masking Truth," hits home. I had my father on a pedestal from infancy on, probably not unlike many other little girls. I thought he was the best, the smartest, the kindest daddy around. I also thought that he would protect and take care of me always.

My father wanted me to keep many secrets. They made me feel important, just between Daddy and me and no one else. I thought I must be special to him when I was told not share our times with anyone, they were only for us. I guess I could say his father mask made me believe that what he was doing was okay. I had often heard, "Honor your father." I just figured this is what fathers were all about, for me this was normal.

I got the idea Mommy also wanted me to keep secrets. My mother taught me well to keep my feelings, thoughts, and voice to myself. So, with her confirming this, I thought this must be what family life was all about. You keep happenings at home to yourself.

My way of handling what was happening was to forget most of the hurtful occurrences. I now know that memory does not truly go away, but it waits to be awakened. My mind would usually dredge up part of a scene when I was feeling low about myself, almost as if to add insult to injury. But as usual, I kept my thoughts to myself. Some of the memories, however, have been with me forever.

When the rest of my childhood memories came bubbling up full bore, I was sure my mother and father would come to my aid and immediately help me through this crisis.

They had been there before when I needed them, so I was sure they would be again. After all, they are my parents and this was by far the most painful thing I had ever been through! I thought they would say that they made a terrible mistake long ago and they were hoping I wouldn't remember. But now that I have, they would want to know how they could help me and make it easier. I wanted them to say that my memories were correct and that I was not stupid after all. Most of all I wanted them to say they were sorry, so very sorry and to please forgive them.

At that point I really needed to hear that they were remorseful. That seemed very important to me then. I thought the word "sorry" would be so healing. It also seemed my forgiving them would come a lot easier if they had spoken their truth. Their silence amazed me.

Through the family grapevine I heard they now deemed me mentally ill. What were they talking about! Don't they remember? I guess you really *don't* tell family secrets. Their silence was clear to me; it spoke volumes. I now know the secrets were not an okay thing, but a sad happening that was occurring inside the confines of my home and family. I had been tricked. How could they? I thought I was loved. I trusted them. I felt betrayed!

I still wonder why I was so trusting as a child. Was I stupid like my dad said or was it just that my circumstances were such that I had to trust them for my survival? Yes, the mother-father mask meant truth to me. How would any tiny child know the difference? How sad it is to be betrayed by your own parents, the ones you entrusted with your security and life.

*"If you could start looking into people, into their eyes and beyond
what they represent to you, you would see their soul."*
Cameron

CHAPTER 5

Removing Pedestals

Cameron

People of great power are often put on pedestals by others. They
are revered. You may think their path is to be followed, something to
be fashioned by. The "shirt-tailers" believe that if they walk in the
path of someone on a pedestal this will add greatness and power to
them. This is a fake power rather than a real power. It is a path only
for that person, no one else. You do little service to people when you
put them above you. That is not what your soul wishes, it is what
your head may wish.

Please don't ever put anyone higher or lower than another person.
You are all perfect—exactly and completely the same. Putting others
on a pedestal is such a grave disservice to their soul. It is important
that you understand this.

It seems as if earth likes to choose people just by coincidence.
Sometimes they go up the ladder of success very quickly. They may
even win the lottery and become more important to others than before,
making them into someone they are not. What a disservice to these
people.

Often people think that rubbing elbows with the wealthy means
they are the same too. That reasoning is only from the head. Heads
are doing that kind of leading, not souls. Bless these precious people
as they go on their path, but do not follow.

Don't adopt anyone else's path by saying, "I will follow, that will be good for me. That will bring me stardom, give me an important name and make me wealthy." This is such an unkindness for both of you. Your soul doesn't want that; it has its own path.

Also be very wary of anyone who wishes to be your leader by saying, "Follow me, and I will give you a feeling that you're more powerful." They may say they have all the answers. But be wary of this. How can that be? How can anyone be better than anyone else? No one was created to be more precious than another.

You do have a choice. When you choose to put others on a pedestal it takes you completely off your path, binding you heavily in your heart-soul area. It is important to stay on your own path. Sometimes your mind draws the conclusion that those on a pedestal are somehow holier. This is often done to people in leadership roles in churches. What a disservice to do to them. They are there to serve God. They are not there to lose themselves but often this is what happens. They have lost themselves in the search for God. People latch onto them and call them special names. Their souls don't like this as it draws too much from them.

Often we see that people placed on pedestals leave earth at an early age. They cannot take the pressure, they are just the same as anyone else; no one is different. If everyone really knew they were equal we would rejoice! A wonderful goal for this total awareness to happen would be in the next two hundred years in earth time. Don't look down or up at someone, just know everyone is equal.

This inequality often happens in business. There always has to be someone who is "head of" and then all the little worker bees underneath. That's the way it is done on earth. The person who is "head of" has so much power. That brings us a sadness because they think they are more powerful, when they are not. Their soul is so lost and they get so confused.

It may surprise you to know that famous and powerful people are often very lonely. It may appear that they have lots of friends, certainly many are vying for their attention, but so often they are actually lonely inside. Famous people have their face splashed all over which creates the illusion that they are much more special than others; these people become revered by many who wish to be like them, thinking then they would be okay. That is so sad for us to see because they are often the loneliest and many are searching the hardest.

People of extremely little means are the ones who are often more connected with themselves. Homeless people are often an example of this. They have no one else but themselves and are one with God. They have not become bound quite so tightly, no one is vying to be in their position.

When you come into the presence of those who have an important name, understand their path is very difficult. Something has pushed them up the ladder before they even knew what happened to them. Their life is such a struggle.

You do a kindness when you see others as equal to yourself, never different, higher or lower. Smile at someone on the street. Smile at a homeless person; look right into their eyes. You may see their beautiful soul. Someone who is dirty, tattered and torn is just as precious as you, or the billionaire. There is no difference whatsoever.

You all have the same beautiful souls. If you could start looking *into* people, into their eyes and beyond what they represent to you, you would see their soul. Soul connections are so important for living life to its fullest. Being connected is very necessary. It is often difficult to connect with people you see on the big screen, because all you see is their outer shell and what they represent to you. In trying to see into another soul you may not get past their shell.

Next we would like to go into the soul connection with others. In order to do that and have you understand the feeling, it would be best if you would look deeply into another person's eyes. You may believe that what they represent to you is not proper but please try. Look beyond their eyes and see their beautiful shining soul. Make a special attempt to look into the eyes of people who you normally would shy away from. If you can, you may find some amazing things would happen.

Carole

For many years I often had my father and mother on a pedestal. When they came crashing down right before my eyes, I felt exposed and scared. It seemed there was no one that I could look to for guidance and security. When I understood that my parents were incapable of being any foundation for me, where could I go? I had to find my own way.

I remember being told frequently as a child that I, or my actions, were stupid. Soon I came to believe it was true. This message was sent in words and through body language. I felt like a failure. In my adult life I couldn't even take off that extra twenty pounds that seemed to plague me. Will I always be a failure? Where will I get my answers? Who will I lean on?

My parents included me as part of the family even with my apparent meager smarts. What now? Did I even have a path waiting for me? It seemed unlikely, as I was already in my late forties, that I could find my path now. How could I ever make a dent in the world? I felt I could never venture out and take a risk because my dad just might be right. How could I expose myself to something new? What if I failed? How long could I pretend that I was just as smart as other people?

Because channeling was so foreign to me it seemed embarrassing. After all, my whole life had already been turned upside down with therapy. How much could my friends and family hear without tiring of my ever-changing life? Cameron and the other spirits became a well-kept secret. Then one day a friend and I were in a deep conversation when I heard Cameron say, "Tell her about me." I hesitated, but after thinking it over, felt comfortable enough to share my secret with this open-minded woman.

The time did seem right. She was mourning the recent loss of her sibling and I hoped Cameron could offer her some comfort. He did indeed come through after she showed an interest in hearing him. I was amazed to find Cameron was able to relay comforting facts about her deceased sibling. He gave my friend the closure she needed in knowing that her sibling was now okay, safe, and happy to be freed of the bondage he made for himself on earth.

Many times since then I have heard Cameron offer, "Tell him or her about me." Now I trust that voice to know that this person will be accepting of Cameron and that a message of paramount healing will come through. Cameron has never failed on this for anyone. I have seen some amazing healing and closure for people from hearing Cameron's words. This is profound to watch and feels right to me now and makes me feel so very blessed.

Cameron tells us he will be around for my healing, the healing of others, and to channel this book. He says his purpose in this book is only to do the spiritual groundwork. Then a spirit of a higher teaching will continue where he left off. I can already feel her presence.

I find that when Cameron does so much healing using my voice, people sometimes think I might have their answers even when I'm not channeling him. Their answers are within them. Channeling comes easily to me. All our gifts come in so many forms. Now I find Cameron hovers close for many of my conversations and often "drops" tidbits of wisdom into my head at appropriate times. I will always continue to credit him when I choose to use his words. We can always find the answers to all our questions in our soul area. We can tap into them at will, just by listening to that little voice.

I see how such a gift as mine can go to your head and might allow one to think they have other people's answers. You may even consider yourself to have extra wisdom due to this ability. Unfortunately, this gift can lead to being put on a pedestal, by yourself or others. For me, that would be frightening and make me feel separate. The pedestal position is not one that would be comfortable for me. It took me so long to find my path of light that to step off that path for some fake glory is unthinkable. The light is leading me in the opposite direction.

*"Soul connection is such a gift for both parties
and can be done by everyone."*
Cameron

CHAPTER 6

Soul Bonding is Freedom

Cameron

Bonding with another soul is the ultimate task we wish to discuss. We find you strive for this often in your life. Soul bonding is the essence of living and is really quite easy. The soul can be seen beyond the eyes if you look *into* the eyes. It appears like a light shining in the fog. It looks somewhat like a light of a ship glistening on the ocean. Look deeply into someone's eyes, going beyond their eyes in order to see their beautiful shining soul.

Soul bonding is available to you at any time. When you soul bond with another, there is a connection that nothing can sever. When talking to others look beyond their mouth and appearance, look deeply into their eyes; there you will get a soul connection with them. When you do this you may feel a sensation in your chest that travels down into your stomach area. It is similar to a shooting wave of energy.

Soul connection is such a gift and can be done by everyone. You will find that we are all connected as one. Everyone is absolutely the same. Only the shells and experiences of people are different. You really are the same, one hundred percent the same. When you recognize this you can break away from your shell and expose yourself for who you are. In fact, we are all the same; there is nothing to hide.

The next time you look into someone's eyes, try not to be embarrassed by staring just an instant longer. Some people have a hard time looking others in the eyes; it brings a blush of embarrassment to them. Why is that? We often find what really happens is that when others look deeply into your eyes you may feel that they can see what you have or haven't achieved or what you are not too proud of. It conjures up feelings of nakedness and exposure. People don't like that feeling.

A good way to start soul bonding would be with a willing friend that you feel comfortable with. Look *deeply* into their eyes and allow yourself to do this for several minutes. Just lose yourself in those beautiful shining jewels; they are so lovely. Look beyond them; think of nothing else around you. See how deeply you can look into their eyes and hunt for that shining light. When you find the light there will come a bonding. The two of you will bond and become one. What a beautiful gift you could give to each other if you would allow this to happen.

We often find that when people walk down crowded streets their eyes look down to the pavement. They do not wish to look into other peoples' eyes. They don't even know that bonding is what would happen if they were to do this. They believe something about them might be shameful, and just don't wish to be exposed.

Some also think if they look straight into someone else's eyes those people may want something from them. There are many other reasons why people don't like to look at each other. Frequently we find that when people are not in truth they will not look anyone in the eyes. Their eyes will dart around to many places. We are sad about that because this is when they are the furthest away from soul connection, far away from connecting to anyone. That is not your purpose on earth. Your soul's desire is to be connected to and with each other.

We see you are striving to find your own beauty and destiny and find out if you are all the same. When you do not look into other's eyes you become isolated and disconnected from them. You are really distancing yourself from God this way since we are all part of the Oneness.

After you have practiced soul bonding with a friend, quite amazing things will happen. You will want to be around them often. You will feel so connected as if you have never felt connected before. Once you have learned this lesson well and are able to put down your guard for just a minute and start looking into the eyes of strangers you will find you are connecting right and left with people.

Sometimes because you are connecting you might think they have more interest in you than before. In the next chapter we give you a bit of caution about this. Do not over emphasize looking into eyes. It does not have to come with any duty attached to it. It is just for the connection of the soul and that is all. This is just for a second and then it is accomplished. You have reconnected with that one. Then you can go on and see other strangers and you both will be okay. It does not mean that you will need to walk a path with everyone whose eyes you look deeply into.

Soul bonding does come with a caution when looking deeply into another's eyes. There are always two sides to everything. If it were not so it would not be balanced. We do not want to put any fear in; that is not the idea at all. More on this subject will be explained later in other chapters. Just know for now that everything has two sides or meanings to it.

It takes a lot of nerve to be able to look squarely in the eye of someone. They may pull back and think, "What does this person want from me? What is it? What are they seeing?" If you get to the point where you can look deeply into their eyes and they do the same to you, then wonderful feelings will happen for both of you.

We would love to observe a unity on earth. It has to start someplace. A good place to start is with eye connection, because that is where the soul can be seen. It brings a good feeling when you can find someone's soul. It also affects every facet of living. People may become disconnected and disjointed from themselves as well as others if they do not find their path of light. Soul bonding can assist them in finding their path. This is a simple exercise that starts small and grows. Much like dominoes it will spread throughout the world. That will be such a joy to us. Bless all of you.

Carole

As far back as I can remember eye contact has always been uncomfortable for me. A few times over the years people have actually said to me, "What's wrong with your eyes?" or "Why are you looking down at my chest?" Sometimes I noticed people glance down at themselves to see what I was looking at. When this happened I felt terrible. I was unaware I was doing this until they reacted to my wandering eyes. I was aware though that looking directly into someone's eyes brought me great mental discomfort. I didn't know why, it just did.

Near the end of my therapy it was discovered that my eye habit started before I was two years old. This had become such a part of me that I was totally unaware of doing it. Small children read body language, especially since words don't have much meaning yet. My habit developed as a method of understanding what situation I was in with my father and others. By looking at their hands I was able to read what was coming. It was really my own safety check.

As I became aware of my habit through therapy, I noticed I did this frequently with strangers, especially men. Sometimes it even happened with friends. This also occurred when I had gone off my self-prescribed diet, feeling they could see my self-disgust with another failed attempt at weight loss.

My therapist suggested that whenever I make eye contact and my eyes feel like they want to drop down, to say to myself, "I am safe now." Making that silent statement helped me so much. Often it takes great strength to keep my eyes up, even now. I have to be conscious of where my eyes are or they will drop, simply out of habit.

A few times over the past years I have felt safe enough to let myself look into and beyond someone's eyes. The feeling was always positive. However, I just shrugged it off thinking that I might have known that person from my past. It was also curious that in that instant of eye contact a feeling of bonding with them occurred. I would bring up that bonding remembrance when I was feeling good about myself. This had only happened a few times in my life up until now.

Cameron had suggested in this chapter that I might like to start soul bonding with a willing partner. Nancy and I decided to do this. First we looked into each other's eyes, then I looked beyond her eyes, I was sure I saw a distant light there. Had a lamp made those tiny yellow spots? No, it was daytime and no lights were on in the house. I did not feel a surge of energy between us, nor did she. I felt sure it was because we had soul bonded long ago. We had such fun doing this that we got the giggles. We decided to practice this on others, wanting to see if we would get that surge in bonding with a stranger.

Every place I went during the next week I tried looking directly into people's eyes, then deeper for just a millisecond longer. I noticed this seemed uncomfortable for a lot of people. Many would shy away but a few did allow me a glance.

When I was able to greet someone's eyes in depth, amazing things happened. I felt a surge of energy and bonding with this person. The surge traveled from my chest to my stomach. It seemed as if we had to sneak one last peek at each other to see what was manifesting.

I have also been practicing by watching people on television. I can stare longer that way without embarrassment. It is easy if they are close up and looking directly into the camera. It was absolutely amazing that I felt the same surge of energy rush inside me. Their eyes became alive right through the television. At that instant I felt such kinship to them and felt so equal even though the screen had a way of making them seem more important. This adventure of eye contact is so freeing and healing for me.

"Eyes can be used in many ways."
Cameron

CHAPTER 7

The Windows of the Soul

Cameron

When you look into someone's eyes, for just half a second longer than usual, a reverence can be reached between the two of you. This does not come with any sort of duty attached to it or any necessity to do something with this person. Nor does it come with a bonding other than a soul bonding. When you look deeply into each other's eyes, so much can be seen especially of the person's past, including their hardships. Sometimes when you connect with someone they may feel that they have done something and wonder why they deserved such a stare. They may be puzzled. People then become a little cautious and may think you want to take something from them that's theirs. And that is not so.

We believe when you have made a soul connection with someone, who has allowed it, that it is best to just leave it at that. It would be our wish that you leave the wonderful connection feeling blessed, for that instant of bonding.

Some people use their eyes to get their way. When people lie to you they often want to look away and do not want to make eye contact with you. The opposite is when someone wants to look into your eyes to gain power over you or intimidate you. This often happens to children by their parents or other adults. Eyes can be used in many ways. Most ways are glorious but some people have devised a system where they can have a great deal of power over others by looking deeply into their eyes to control them. The recipient of this almost becomes a puppet to them. This is where our caution comes in. Do not be a party to this if someone wants to look into your eyes and bond for a special purpose for them. You do not need to reciprocate in any way.

We cannot in any way caution children about an adult's desire to look into their eyes and take advantage of them. This is a problem we see on earth. There is really no way to warn these small ones. We are speaking to adults and believe as generations continue the adults will pass this on to their children. We hope they will say, "Be cautious of those who look you in the eye *if* they have a devious deed behind it." You may think you need to glance at someone as a way of honoring them and there is truth in that, but if their look makes you not feel right in your heart-soul area, look away. Your statement could be, "No, you will not take part of me with you. You will not overtake me with the power of your eyes."

We often see small ones becoming intimidated, much like a puppy would be, following those who have drawn them in by eye contact. This brings us great sorrow. This is where there is confusion. The eyes can be used for perfection or the opposite. Be a little wary of this when you look into someone's eyes. We do think in times to come you will be able to recognize this.

Sometimes you might see a frightening intensity in someone's eyes. This is because they have a desired purpose for themselves and you cannot see their soul for it is bound too tightly. The window of their soul behind their eyes has almost closed. Their devious purposes have done this. We do not want to scare or put any fear into anyone but do want you to be cautious about this. We are not saying, in any way, that there is not a soul in everyone. If a person is open, you will be able to see their soul.

Soul bonding is a beautiful thing to do. We hope you will be able to practice this a little bit. Remember that just because you soul bond it does not mean you have a duty to that person or they have a duty to you. The problem we see on earth is that many people no longer look into or beyond another's eyes. It seems to be a big fear. People often think that something is expected of them or vice versa.

There are some in whom, when you look into their eyes, no soul can be seen. These people do things only for their own concern and their own greatness. They need to find the path of light so their soul can show through their windows. Please let's all bless them and put them in our care, for one day you will look into their eyes and the windows will be open. You will see their soul. We will delight in that.

There are some people that you may not want any particular contact with, such as homeless street people or beggars. They may say, "Please give me money, I have no job or home." If you look deeply into their eyes you will most likely see a beautiful soul. We can almost guarantee it. You will bond with them. It is wonderful for you to see that. You do not need to feel sorry for these people. They have chosen this path. We do know that for them to sit on the street corner seems like a challenge to you, but in fact, it is not as difficult a challenge to them. This is something they have chosen. We bless them highly in their chosen life. You can learn a lot from these people. If you can look into and beyond their eyes, you will be absolutely amazed at the shining you will see there. We do not believe they will shun you either, as you might think. You will be very surprised. Often we see their souls are not bound quite so tightly. They have asked for a hard mission and they *are* doing it well.

It is not our intention to put any kind of fear in you but just know that eyes can be used for so much. Eyes are beautiful windows to the soul. However, if you look into someone's eyes and can't see their soul, or anything except hurt, bless them especially. They need to have their windows open and you can help do that with your blessing. We do not want to convey that you need too much caution with eye bonding. Just be aware of all that can manifest when you look into another's eyes.

Carole

The "Windows of the Soul" added a whole new dimension to eyes that I had not explored before. When I look into someone's eyes, fear comes from inside me as to what they are going to see. I never thought of the possibility that some would want to overtake me with their power. I had to replay many childhood scenes to be able to recognize that my offenders *never* looked me squarely in the eye. I realize now that I cannot recall with absolute certainty, the color of my parents' eyes.

I cannot ever remember looking deeply into anyone's eyes in our household as I was growing up, just a quick glance seemed the way it was. Shame may have prevented this. I guess somehow if I did not see what was happening I could block it out easier as a child. That would also seem true for my betrayers. Placement of the hands and tone of voice became much more important to me than eyes. The thought of this makes me sad that I was not able to look my offenders squarely in the eyes and say, "No, you cannot take part of me with you!" The opportunity to do this has long passed. The hope of the future for our little ones makes me excited. How wonderful that if in many years to come, children could learn that eyes are for soul bonding, transference of love, and seeing the beauty all around them.

"Each person is as precious as another."
Cameron

CHAPTER 8

Protecting Your Soul's Light

Cameron

We would like to bless those who are seeking the truth and light from you and others. We know that their path will be easier by your sharing with them, and that is good. When they find their own path and their own light, they can do the same for others. Each person is as precious as another.

As you open up to people and soul bond with them, they can become quite attracted to you and you to them. They are drawn to you, as if you have charisma. Sometimes we see people in great need wanting a part of you, wanting much of your light. A concern comes when they take too large a part. They would not mean to hurt you in any way but they can take too much of your light and energy.

We would like to suggest that when you are in the presence of someone who is wounded or needy be aware if they are causing some mental exhaustion for you. They may say, "Give me advice on this" or "Please share your thoughts with me on that." Although they love to hear your words, notice if after such a conversation you feel very tired. Large groups or crowds of people can also have a draining effect. It is necessary to hold your precious soul light inside of you, not letting it go, but letting it shine through to others. It can be seen in your eyes and can also radiate from your body to others. They can feel it. This is why it needs to be protected.

Your soul is like a beautiful sparkler radiating its light. To protect your light you need only visualize a piece of clear glass surrounding you. Your soul's light can radiate its glowing beauty to others, yet it is protected by the glass. This is a way of guarding yourself from those who would tend to unknowingly drain your light, whether it would be individuals or crowds. Practicing this visualization when around others will assist you. In this way you will keep the divine presence within you radiating as it is meant to do.

It is important not to give away your light, as that would not be fair to either party. Everyone has to find their own light and their own path. To give it away is not a kindness for either one of you. Once you have found your light, protect it as if it's a shining jewel.

Carole

Often when I have done a reading for someone with Cameron, our conversations turn into a great spiritual interchange. I love these special times with my friends. I have noticed that Cameron hovers around for most of the conversation and drops a few tidbits into my head to enhance our exchange. These times are very easy for me; the words just seem to be on the tip of my tongue. I thank Cameron so much for helping to enlighten my words. Lately I have noticed that I wish to carry on such conversations when he is not hovering quite so closely. It seems I desire to have more and more spiritual connections with others. It's amazing how people keep coming into my life.

I do find though, after such conversations, that I seem a little weary. According to Cameron that seems to mean I have unprotected light showing through. How exciting for me to think that I have something to give to others and they to me. I shall again practice arming myself with the cylinder to protect my precious light. Cameron also used the words "angel film" when he first taught me this technique. I have often used it with good results but lately I must have been taking it for granted or just forgotten. The reminder is just what I needed!

"You have all your answers inside of you."
Cameron

CHAPTER 9

Tapping the Peace Within You

Cameron

When you find your peace you will be able to generate it to many others. It is like a ripple effect, one to another. This is what it is all about. We would love to see peace on earth in the next two hundred years or so.

Most of the time you are able to look into someone's eyes and see their soul. But if for some reason you cannot, try to look beyond their hurt or hiding. For it is there and you will, in time, see their soul. This may take several exchanges before you see their soul but be patient, it is there, if you continue to look. Often we see those who hide behind a defensive shield. They think they are unworthy or not as precious as others and will not allow their soul to be seen. Know that there is a soul within all people.

The soul shines like a rare diamond in a jewelry store. Many people on earth find diamonds and jewels very precious. But there is nothing as precious as your soul. Once you have come to an understanding of this and feel that what you have inside of you is precious and revered, your life will be beautiful.

Do you remember when we talked about the fan? If you were to remain with your fan open and the windows to your soul open your life would then be miraculous. We wish for all of you to find your reverence and beauty. We are proud of all of you, for we know it is not an easy path on earth.

When you distance yourself from God, you are really not happy.

Some say, "Well, I don't believe in God, I don't believe in anything, any sort of source different than myself. I am the best. I am the one." As people say that to themselves their soul doesn't believe it. Their head is getting involved in this. Try to understand and bless those who speak of no God, no light, nothing spiritual. It is sad for us to think that some believe when you die you just fall into a black hole of some sort.

We observe that some churches want to put fear in people by saying, "If you are not good you will go to hell. If you are good you will go to heaven." But what is good? Exactly what is it and who makes the rules? Are they earth rules? Just who decides who is good and who is bad? We see that everyone is good and precious. Their circumstances control where they are. That is really all it is.

If you really choose your circumstances then you can also choose to be one with God, one with the light, one with the source of all that is loving, if you wish to be one with this, it is necessary to go with your fan wide open. At every turn, every corner, be sure your fan is open. If it is closed at all, don't make that turn. Reflect; see what that corner has to tell you when the fan is closing. If you continue to always follow your fan, it would be absolutely certain that the windows of your soul would be open in a very short time.

The eyes are the windows of the soul but often you cannot see through them into the soul. If you could visualize shutters that open and close behind your eyes, you would have a good picture of a human protective device. When an individual is in fear the shutters close, to prevent viewing of the soul. When an individual is in truth the shutters open and the soul is seen.

Remember also that all of you have your answers within. You do not need anyone else for any of your answers. They are all stored right inside of you. By remembering these concepts you will be following the light and your path. When you allow an open fan and open shutters, all will be able to see your beautiful light and feel your wisdom.

There are those who say, "I don't know how to find my path. I don't know where I am going in life. What am I here for?" If they could keep their fan and shutters wide open there would no longer be any question because their path will come to them. One cannot help but find their path that way, as they will be directed right to it.

Keep practicing the fan and shutter techniques and when you are confident you may wish to pass it on to others. Just tell them to follow their heart, follow their heart-soul area. All the answers are within them. If they were to follow with their fan open for a while, the windows to their soul will also flap open. Then they will know their wholeness and find their path. People will not need to grab and take from others, as they will have their own answers.

You are on your path when you keep your fan and shutters open. In this way every answer or decision comes clearly and effortlessly from within you. For those who are searching, we know it is scary. You may think, "I can't answer these myself. I have to ask this person or that person because I know they have great wisdom." When you do that, it pulls from them a bit. It also keeps you off your path. While it is good to have an exchange with a friend it is best, however, to have a two-way exchange. Doing soul bonding would get your world into a peaceful frame of mind. You can start this today. This may seem very simple but life *is* simple. People can make life so complicated.

Carole

I find myself in a situation that is very foreign to me. I know all this could have been avoided if I had only listened to my inner guidance. I find myself taking a man to small claims court to recapture monies due me. The money does not seem nearly as important to me as trying to stop him from doing the same thing to other unsuspecting people. Upon investigation, I learned he does this as a practice. I am just one in a long line of people seeking what's due them.

We often vacation with our children and their families. These are special times for us. Normally I make arrangements for these trips by working with a rental agency. We have never been disappointed in our accommodations.

For this spring break, a different type of scenery seemed in order. I scanned the newspapers and made a lot of calls. I found a home offered by a private party that seemed to fit our needs. I talked to a very pleasant gentleman. The house sounded perfect; everything we wished for in a rental seemed to be there and more. But something felt strange. However, I shrugged my feelings off. Weeks before our arrival I sent him the final payment, which was a very foolish thing to do.

Within a few days I began to have more strange feelings about this man and the house that I had just rented. I called him to obtain a little more information and found his phone was disconnected. Funny, I had just spoken to him five days before at that number. I only had a post office box address for him. What now? Was my vacation house and money gone? I was feeling very unsettled and felt so silly for not checking the house out further. Why was I so trusting? I wanted to believe in him. In one of our conversations this man had told me he was trustworthy. Why would he feel he had to tell me that, because he was not? What to do now? It really seemed too late to find another rental on such short notice.

In a few days the man called me and explained why his phone was no longer in service and gave directions to his rental house. Silly me, all was well. Why did I even question the gnawing feeling inside of me? Everything seemed okay now.

Spring break was here. Everything was packed into four cars: kids, skis, golf clubs, tennis rackets and more. We were on our way! The rental house was very secluded off the highway, down a winding gravel road, deep into the woods. As I spotted the large house in the clearing, a jolt went through me and I began to feel nervous. Stepping into the house I felt my heart begin pounding. As we were unpacking I started feeling sick to my stomach. My daughter said the same thing was happening to her. We all stopped what we were doing and looked around. We were not sure what made the energy so bad in that house. It was filthy and hadn't been cleaned in many months.

Cockroaches and spiders called it home.

The children said they wanted to leave. My grandson said he felt unsafe. Spending the night there, much less sleeping in the beds, seemed unthinkable. To us this house was definitely uninhabitable and very misrepresented. About that time the owner called to see if all was well. We told him our plight. He seemed most surprised, embarrassed, apologetic, and understanding and would send us a complete refund within the week. We have yet to see a penny. That was months ago.

The rush for all of us to get out of there astonished me. The cars were packed in record time. I felt energy of such strong strength that it almost pushed me out the door. Amazing! Where to go to now? We were fortunate to find a house available for the week at our favorite resort, which housed our twelve people. The opening, I am sure, was not by chance.

I carried the black energy pit in my stomach, as did my daughter, for several hours. Upon arriving at our destination, I hit a pole and shattered the back window of my van. Lessons were taught hard that week, but I hope I learned them well. I now know that I must always listen to my inner voice and feelings. Going only with my fan open during the search for our vacation house would have brought me peace instead of such an unsettling experience.

Two months later brought a conclusion to this story. I was not given the opportunity to meet this man personally in court as I had hoped. He defaulted on responding in the prescribed time to our claim against him. We were sent papers signed by the judge stating that we now have the right to claim our money through his bank account, attach his wages or even put a lien on his property. These options came up empty. As I scurried around with the judgment in hand to try for a different form of collection, I felt tightness in my chest. It became apparent to me something was not feeling right.

I stood somewhat reluctantly in the long Department of Motor Vehicles office line to get a printout on his many cars. It was curious but I realized that I did not want to have his cars impounded and sold after all. The thought of doing this gave me a sad feeling. Even though

I knew monies owed me would certainly come back to me when the cars were auctioned off.

It was finally my turn at the counter. I requested owner information printouts from the Department of Motor Vehicles clerk. As she was handing me the papers I felt a profound shift stirring inside me. I knew I did not want to pursue this case any longer. A new strength and peacefulness filled me.

What was happening? My head kept trying to make sense and reason with that big feeling inside of me that said, "Drop this case!" The feeling was so strong that this time I listened, giving it validity. Were my lessons really over? "But you don't have your money yet," yelled my head. After some reflecting I knew that my lessons were at a conclusion and they had been priceless!

I made a list of what I had learned:

1. Follow only with my fan open. If I had done that in the beginning, none of this would have happened.

2. Developed my strong side to pursue the case through the courts. Now I know that I have a strong side to tap into if needed.

3. I realized it is not my duty to save others from this man's ways, nor was it my job to help him find his path. I now know we all must do this for ourselves.

4. I learned to give myself credence when I sensed that it was time to quit chasing all the avenues of payback. I know I can trust this feeling in any situation now.

When I felt my fan closing, I needed to stop what I was doing and take note. In this situation I knew it meant to move on. The money is no longer an issue for me as I realize it was the vehicle to my priceless lessons. Since dropping this claim my fan is wide open and I feel wonderful!

Cameron suggested long ago that I add this happening to the book. I remember balking at the idea as I thought it "petty earth stuff" and I was not particularly proud that I had gotten myself wrapped up in it. Cameron's gentle suggestion came up again after he dictated this chapter. After pondering, I decided to write the story; little did I know, it was packed with so many profound lessons for me. Thank you Cameron!

"Miracles are not for a chosen few, they can happen to you.
You just have to believe."
Cameron

CHAPTER 10

Your Path of Miracles

Cameron

When you are able to go through life with the shutters in back of your eyes and the fan in your heart-soul area open, miracles then come to you. People often think that miracles are just for a certain lucky few. Miracles are often explained away as either being from the hand of God, having a scientific explanation or merely coincidence. Miracles are explained in terms the mind can understand. We offer the concept to you that miracles can happen to you daily, if you are open to them.

Miracle really means something joyous or incredible has happened. People may say, "Oh, I haven't been sick in so long; it's a miracle." But it is not a miracle, this only means they have not pulled illness into them. If you remain on your path, with your fan and shutters open, you cannot help but be healthy. Illness is quite wide spread on earth. It distracts people, while consuming their thoughts and bodies.

Illness is very important to some people. It gets them what they want. Illness can also be a form of control. That seems strange, doesn't it? You can control others by your own illness because others have to give their time to you. They often step off their own path to serve you when you are ill. Usually this is done out of guilt. It is sad to see this pattern so often on earth.

It would be a kindness if people would not so frequently explain their illnesses to others. Hearing so much about your health doesn't do anything for the other person. Why would you burden others constantly by telling them, "I have this hurt, that problem, I picked up the flu," and on and on? Some people get so into the mode of illness as being a way to get attention that it becomes a habit and then don't know how to get out of the cycle. Their soul does not want to be ill.

Your body does not need to hurt and ache. When you find your path, illness will not be a part of you. As if a miracle had happened you say, "Here I am, eighty years old, yet no illness. Why am I not ill?" The simplest answer is that you are on your path and it does not allow any illness to be a part of you.

People often die from major illnesses. It's not that their body wants to get sick or suffer, but that their soul wants to be free of this life. What is this thing called illness? In your creation the plan was to die easily just like going to sleep, when all your lessons are done.

People used to live longer in biblical times. Today we often see babies born with a disease or deformity. How can a baby have a terrible disease? Have you ever wondered about that? What did they ever do to deserve this? With the information we are giving you this doesn't make much sense, does it? When babies come to this life with an illness they are trying to deal with things from a past life. They have made a conscious choice to do this and live out their illness. Even as a tiny infant they are learning so much in their soul.

Some young people draw to themselves an illness and leave earth early, by earth standards. One reason for this may be that they were drawing from a past life. Another may be that they decided to draw an illness into themselves to help teach someone close to them, or others, a lesson about illness. It might also be that earth is so harsh for them that they draw illness to them as an escape route.

If you had your fan and shutters open there would be no need for illness. Then what would the doctors do? What would hospitals do if this were really so? This is a big concern, isn't it? We see that earth has been very affected by the medical field. Consider the possibility that in two hundred years or so, illness would be obsolete and that there would be no need for medical services! How could that be? At this time illness is such a big part of the earth that it stretches the mind to think that it could possibly happen.

Hopefully a very tiny seed is planted to think about this possibility. Perhaps then when a negative thought comes into your mind such as, "Maybe I will get that illness," you can replace it with a positive happy thought. Try it and see what happens, feel how your body responds.

We do not see that there will be a big change on earth in illness in the next two centuries. When it does happen though, people will have to read about illness in the history books. This will happen. It seems strange now because illness is such a big part of your world today. Perhaps some of you reading or listening to this will have the opportunity to come back to earth in a few hundred years and see how it is. It will be a different world; we can guarantee that! We are excited about the future of no illness on earth, for us that would be a miracle.

Miracles can happen. They can happen in your body by freeing you of illness or releasing you from physical or mental pain. Often when we see people with a serious illness or handicap such as not being able to walk, and then suddenly they are able to walk, people say, "It's a miracle." That is not really what is happening at all.

What's happening is their soul says, "I will not accept this illness anymore. I will get rid of it." So you use the word "miracle" since it means so much. Many think a miracle is something that can *only* occur from an outside source. In other words, something outside of you has to have caused it. God, Jesus, others, or other things are usually credited with these miracles.

Understand that the miracles are *in you*. They are not coming from outside. They are coming via God, but God is in all of you, every one of you. We are all connected. Some think if miracles come from outside your body, then Jesus must have done it. How could that be so? Jesus is the same as you. You are as capable. Do you see what we are saying? Miracles begin in you, become one with you and can happen daily.

If you ask for something with a deep desire, it will happen and become a part of you, if this is for the good of your soul. You do not have to wait for miracles to happen from outside your body. Miracles are not just for a chosen few, they can happen to you. When you are on your path, with your fan and shutters open, miracles happen constantly. We would like to leave you with the thought that: *You are a miracle*.

Carole

My self-assigned job for Part 1- "Awakening" was to take the cassette tape on which Cameron has dictated the chapter, insert it into a player with headphones and transfer his words longhand onto paper. Although this is sometimes tedious and time consuming, I love this job because I can really get in touch with Cameron's words.

Channeling these chapters is different than doing a reading for someone. When Cameron is dictating I hear no conversations among the spirits, nor see any pictures nor pick up any feelings. I am not interacting in my mind with the words he is speaking. I remember little of what he says; for with no pictures for my memory to draw upon, everything seems blank. I feel like I am on a journey each time I put the headphones to my ears.

As I was listening and writing the words of this chapter, chills came over me. I'm amazed at how healing his words are for me. Exposing the hidden parts of my mind is so freeing. As far back as I can remember illness and operations were a big part of my world. They made me feel important and cared for. This started at the age of six and lasted until I was in my late forties. It's a little embarrassing and hard to admit that I looked forward to being in the hospital. The very first thought that crossed my mind upon entering was that I would be taken care of and my mother would visit, bringing me flowers.

Many of my earlier emotional needs were not met, but somewhere in my being, her hospital visits seemed to make up for some of this and brought me comfort. Creating kidney stones was my vehicle to be admitted for care. Hospitals take this condition seriously and act swiftly. I loved the attention. The degree of pain made no difference to me, people were responding to my needs.

As the years passed, the kidney stones were just part of the long list of conditions within my body. I could claim quite a collection of operations and illnesses by my late forties. Some days my body just seemed to be filled with aches and pains. Maybe this happens when you are nearing fifty. My parents certainly have had their share of illnesses. I thought it just ran in the family.

When I started my therapy I had claimed a long list of bodily ills. What amazes me to this day is that as my childhood memories bubbled up, my ills began to disappear. My last operation was a curious one, removing a very large boil on my toe. As I entered the hospital for this last trip under the knife my body seemed to be boiling over. Was it my trapped memories? They emerged with rapid succession in the next few weeks. This seems very profound to me.

It was interesting for me to learn that I did not have to feel old or be sick just because I was in middle age. I can now see that I have no need for any illness. The thought of ever having an operation seems foreign now. I do know if I ever call an illness into me again I will question myself as to why I pulled it into my energy and for what purpose.

Near the end of my therapy and for two years afterwards I had not one ache, pain, or illness of any sort. A miracle had happened! I did have to readjust my thoughts to the fact that illness no longer served a purpose for me. I was getting used to being pain-free and felt so wonderful and alive.

Then it happened. Nearly one year ago today I had a stroke, then hours later I had another. As I lay in the emergency room of the hospital, I felt like I was in slow motion. My speech was slurred; motor skills were poor with both sides of my body affected and short term memory dulled. It seemed that everyone was behind several sheets of glass. Everything seemed so untouchable. Is this what it feels like when you are dying? The possibility of another stroke may be imminent the doctors said. That did not happen and I was sent home.

Speech, occupational, and motor skills therapists would be sent to my home when I was strong enough. How could this be? I was fifty-one years old and wanted no part of illness. Why did I have these strokes? I thought I finally had my life on a path that did not seek doctors and hospitals. What happened?

As the months droned on at home I struggled to eat with a spoon and fork, use a pencil, curl my hair, brush my teeth, and color in the lines. I learned to walk and talk all over again. The more I learned, the more I realized what a miracle these strokes had been for me. I was learning all the skills a child learns at home but this time I was in a loving, nurturing environment and not in dysfunctional surroundings. I needed to redo my childhood through the loving hands of these therapists. What a gift this was for me.

What I learned so deeply became valuable lessons for me. I have patience with those who cannot speak at a pace I think necessary. I don't stare at someone who cannot walk without a wavering stride. I do not talk over those who have slurred speech and won't pretend they are not there. I became aware. I have been in a body such as this and the stares cut deep. The upturned eyes of impatience were so deflating for me. The most precious gift that I learned from this was when I deemed myself useless, my husband, children, and grandchildren saw me as whole and showed me their unconditional love. It still brings me great joy and awe to think how my strokes helped me to find my path of wholeness.

The doctors are unsure what caused the strokes. One of the many possibilities is that years of stress can cause certain areas to constrict at the base of the brain stem. All I need to know is that one year later I have come full circle in my healing with a new awareness. Within six months I had my "wheels" back. My first venture on the freeway was mind-boggling. *Where* was everyone going and *why* were they going so fast? It made little sense. I felt there must be more important things in life than just scurrying around. But soon I became part of the flow of traffic. I had to keep up! For six months I was able to go at my pace and not the pace that traffic or anything else demanded. Part of me longs for that again. I have now been reacquainted with my tennis racket and have just taken up golf lessons. I am back to full activity.

It may be interesting to note that Cameron would not speak through me for the many months I was recuperating. He did however, let me know that he would watch over me, hover close and return to channeling when I was stronger. When I had sufficient strength Cameron came through as promised and said the strokes were a necessary part of my healing. I had drawn them into me. I feel truly blessed to have learned my lessons this way. For me, it was a miracle!

"Balance is upset when people are in fear."
Cameron

CHAPTER 11

Balancing Your Energies

Cameron

Can you think about a circle that would have two sides to it? A circle is a continuous thing, isn't it? How could it have two opposite sides? Does this seem a bit confusing?

You have an agreement in your body for your male and female energies to become whole. No matter what sex you are, you have both male and female energy. Does that make sense to you? You have to be both to become one.

On earth it seems people want to clearly be either male or female. They cannot understand how you could have both energies. To them it doesn't make sense, but each energy does compliment the other, thus creating wholeness.

Think of two energies: one strong, one soft. Which do you think of as male and which as female? Most people think of the female energy as soft and the male as strong. An allowed softer energy would bring a balance to the male. Many people think of the female as soft and needing to be taken care of by the male. How could they be whole if they are taken care of by others?

To be a complete whole you have to have a balance of each, half male and half female. Balance is what you gasp for, as if to take in air. The balance is supreme. It is upset when people are in fear. They think the only way out of their fear is to be controlling. When they do this they adopt a male energy. They believe this gives them a lot of strength and power, but underneath it all there is fear.

62

The feminine side is often described as a deferring energy that allows a stronger energy to take care of things. If one energy is stronger than the other, where is the balance? What do you get out of life when you let others make decisions for you? You must not let anyone push or shame you into their decisions, even though they think their choices are better for you.

If you went with your fan open you would never have to be strong, weak, or adopt a male or a female energy. Strong or weak, male or female energy is really just an illusion of your mind. We do not see males as any stronger or females as any weaker. We see them as absolutely the same. Male energy may have certain properties that the female energy does not, but they compliment each other. It is not meant that one energy overpowers the other.

We see many women on earth become very weak. They may feel they can't do something because it is a male thing. Who made up these rules? Who says this is a male thing or a female thing? When you buy into that it makes that part of your energy very weak. We do not see any reason why male or female energy is any different at all. The male muscles are structured differently from the females in the physical. One might think if the muscles and bodies are different then the work might be different. That may be so, however, to map your life in only one energy, male or female, does not bring you full circle. There must be a balance.

It has become apparent to us that some think a man must run your country because he is stronger. How can that be? Everyone started out the same. The male-female seed of light is the same, neither one is stronger. Only the male body is, that is all. We see that women are not honored in some countries. Do you think that you might see a female running the United States and some other male-dominated countries in the years ahead? That would bring equality to women.

How could you achieve a balance? How can you all love each other and be one if you are not in balance? Due to the fact that the male has a stronger body the earth has adopted him as a stronger person, some even believe a better person. Why is that? Do you think you could possibly change that? Some of the problem is women often *allow* this to happen. They allow men to take the forefront because they believe that they are weaker and let the male make the decisions. This is not the desire of your soul.

In marriage we often see there is an unconscious agreement based on human heritage that the male should prevail because he is thought to be the stronger and wiser. Could women honor and revere themselves enough to see that they too can make wise decisions? Can men honor themselves enough to realize that a decision made by two is stronger?

There needs to be reform in the work place. Men usually get paid more than a woman for equal positions and are promoted faster. How can that be equal? This says that women are less than men. How can that be? The thinking of equality needs to go into the work place. Some women do succeed in the work place and gain power. However, then we often see women of great power are disliked. Why is that? Don't you like their strength? This needs to be examined further. This is a tiny seed of thought.

Presently men are the pillars of earth; everyone needs to be a pillar, their own pillar. For everyone to achieve wholeness there must be a change in thoughts. To begin this process could you teach your children that women are as precious as men and men as precious as women, no less, no more. Why is it that women should have softer qualities? Do you think they can be more emotional? Some people believe that men should not be emotional. Why should men be robbed of that aspect of themselves, or be shunned for that? We often see fathers teaching their sons to be strong and tough. How could you change that? You must allow males to *feel* all their feelings and females to feel their inner strength.

For everyone to find their potential they must have a totally equal male-female side to them. Everyone must experience all their feelings. Everyone is just as precious as everyone else, male or female. We would like to state that men and women are absolutely the same. We are all full circle. There is no difference whatsoever.

Carole

All my life I have thought the male was the stronger one, not just in body but in mind as well. I always felt I could rely on the male in my life to take care of me. This was especially true with my father. In the early years our whole family relied on him for support and answers. Now that I think back, this must have been very scary for him. With his passing I understand now that he may have felt weak and afraid.

No wonder he became my betrayer. I thought I needed to be weak because I was born female. In turn, he took the power I gave him and filled the shoes I assigned him. It's as if he had to take control of me to exhibit his "fake" strength not to let me down. How very sad. We both lost out.

I wonder how many times during my childhood I heard at home and in church, "Honor your father; honor your mother." Since I was obedient I did what I thought I should do and thus gave much of my power away.

Through much of my lifetime, I gravitated to people who seemed to be stronger than me. Life seemed simpler that way. I let others make all the decisions; it seemed familiar and more comfortable. Long ago I convinced myself that my opinions held little credence, so I adopted the policy of not caring much about anything. The truth is, I really did care.

During therapy I realized that I did have a right to an opinion, just as much right as anyone else. But I was still afraid of confrontations and hurting someone's feelings if I were to disagree with them. It was a slow process for me to make a shift and take risks with another person. I've come to the conclusion that the sharing of different opinions allows thoughtful respect between both parties. This is the opposite of what I feared. If I feel good about the risk, my fan will be wide open in my heart-soul area. When I do share my opposing views I always seem to come though the exchange empowered.

Channeling and writing this book feels expanding. I know there will be some naysayers and that's okay. I am gathering so much strength by doing this and it feels so right, that I will continue on. Cameron's words are wise and given with love, however some things could stir up criticism. For a time I wanted to go back to my old ways. There I knew I could be safe and far from controversy. I know how to be weak and go into a cocoon. How could I possibly hold my own against those with greater knowledge and credentials? What could I back my inner knowing up with?

It took time, but I learned that I could trust my heart.

I feel I am connecting with my male energy that has been asleep. Now I feel secure in this new feeling of wholeness and expansion. It is amazing that I thought my strength came from others. I now understand that achieving wholeness via male and female equality helps bring us all onto our path of light.

"For everything living, there is a cycle in its path toward wholeness. This cycle serves a purpose."
Cameron

CHAPTER 12

Opposites Equal Wholeness

Cameron

What does this title mean, does it seem a play on words? What it means is that for anything to be whole it must have an opposite side to it. What could that possibly mean? How could that suggest anything but nonsense? Actually it is an important concept in achieving wholeness.

In life you are striving to have everything become whole. The only way for something to become whole is to have two sides, but they must be the exact reverse of each other: hard to soft, hot to cold, angry to happy, fearful to calm. What does that all mean? If you look into the dictionary it certainly doesn't say these words have the same meaning.

Often young children say something that seems clear, but they actually mean the exact opposite. They might say, "I'm tired, I want to go home." Yet when you take them home, they run around non-stop. They weren't really tired at all. They were only tired of where they were. However the reverse of tired is energetic. From one end of the spectrum to the other covers it all, thus it is whole.

To become whole everything has to have two meanings, two sides or opposites. That is true of the male and female energies, as explained before. Now, however, we are talking about everything in your entire world. Everything that you can think of must have two sides to it.

As an example, for a beautiful rose to grow and become whole, it has to open up, wither, and then die. This is the complete life cycle of a rose. Does this mean to live is to die? Yes, you are not whole until you are born and later die. You cannot be whole until you die and go on. When you die in your world it is not really death. You never die. You are reborn and reborn and reborn forever, for eternity. There is no death.

When a puppy is born it is cute, sweet and cuddly. The puppy then grows up to be an adult. Sometimes circumstances and consequences create a very angry dog that bites. It's not happy and shows a fierce side. It is exhibiting its wholeness by showing both of its sides, the sweet puppy and the angry dog. The dog would not be whole unless it had experienced, in some way, these different elements.

It is the same with humans. You have to experience all the differences to become whole. What would it be like if you went through life smiling all the time, never a frown or conflict, just smiling? You would learn very little from life this way. What if you went through life saying, "I don't care. I don't have an opinion about anything." What would happen? What part of you would miss out this way? You need to experience both, having an opinion and not having an opinion, for wholeness.

Throughout life there has to be a flip side. How would you know what a possession was if you've never had anything? How would you know you are rich unless you were without money first? It goes back and forth. You have to experience one to have the other for wholeness. Money does not make you complete at all. How can you appreciate anything unless you've had the opposite side of it? You always need to have an opposite viewpoint to get a proper perspective. Appreciation of wellness comes from knowing illness. We are not saying you have to become ill to be whole but you need at least some knowledge of the experience from your present or past lives to know what people are talking about. That goes not just illness but for everything.

Let's look at the grades you receive in school. If you get a high grade, an A, you feel very good and elated. But the next time you get the opposite of an A, an F, a failing grade. Does an A mean you're good and an F, you're bad? To us nothing is ever a failure. To become whole you must experience or have an understanding that everything has two opposite sides in its wholeness. Everything has a different side, its opposite side.

To achieve the ultimate in wholeness it is necessary to come to earth and later return to our side. You go back and forth living so many experiences. Many also believe that when you die you are gone. The opposite is really true. You must die to be reborn, then reborn to die.

When you look at a butterfly, realize how much it goes through. First it is a caterpillar, then it must spin a cocoon around itself and grow there, finally it must break out of the cocoon to become a butterfly. It is transformed in this process. When it is time for the butterfly to leave, its time will be up and it will be gone. Without it being gone, it never really was. It has to be a complete circle to be whole. This is the only way it is.

When you see someone who is angry or a situation that makes you tense, you may not want to be around them. Understand that they were only showing one side of themselves. People cannot be whole unless they find their soft side, their "un-angry" side too. Without anger and soft sides they would not be whole. The two sides achieve a balance.

Knowing this should bring some compassion when you see things happening around you. You may not want to judge people, or things, as freely when you understand that you are seeing only part of a cycle. Everyone you see on earth will come into complete wholeness, whether it is this life or another. Don't judge how they are when you see them. It is very important to get this concept. We wish for this to make sense for you; that *everything is in a cycle when you see it.*

Older people, especially those in a home for the aged, do not get much credence. Many believe their usefulness is gone. The opposite is true. You are just seeing them in a certain cycle in their life. Look deeper with compassion.

When you see someone showing you their undesirable side, know that they also have an opposite side within them. They can achieve that side by going on their path and reclaiming their soul. You're always going to see an opposite to something, just be aware that the cycle you see someone in is *ever changing*. They may be different just within a few minutes. Observe this. It is a kindness not to judge others or animals. Don't even judge tiny flies that bother you by wanting to get into your food. Even they have a time when they would not be a pest to you.

For everything living, there is a cycle in its path toward wholeness. *This cycle serves a purpose.* If you see someone doing something inappropriate in your view, before judging and avoiding them, just know they are in their cycle as you are. Bless them for where they are. Bless them for their anger. Bless them for their yelling. To see a young child being yelled at is disconcerting. Realize that the person yelling is not all anger. They are capable of compassion and love. Realize that the child at a deeper level has asked for the situation.

If you see a situation where you think someone seems out of control with another, bless it. We are aware of it. This does not mean that if you see someone being seriously harmed or a child who is being severely ridiculed that you shouldn't intervene. We are not saying that you shouldn't intervene when someone is in danger, but when you see anger, observe before you judge. Observe and assess the situation. If you need to step in, fine, but some things take care of themselves.

We are aware of all happenings on earth. Be assured that everyone's angels and guides are always monitoring harshness. You will know when someone is in danger and it *is* time and necessary to step in.

Carole

The title, "Opposites Equal Wholeness," seems such a contradiction to me. I then looked down to step into my car and noticed I was standing on bark dust. Then I noticed the tree next to the curb. That was it. I felt it! The tree and the bark dust are in different forms but they are the same.

My awareness opened and as I drove home everything I saw became a lesson for me. I had fun seeing which cycle something was in. I really enjoyed figuring out how things started and in what form they were in. Everything's purpose seemed more magnified to me.

When I started applying this theory to people, I felt such compassion. As I continued into the week, I would see people in their angry mode and just knew that inside them was also softness. I found no need to stare or get upset at their unsettled state.

My deep healing, though, came with my father. I believe it would be quite a surprise to people who knew him that he did have a side other than what his public face was. It's sad to note that his loving, calm side could have an unsettled flip side to it. Now I see he was trying so hard to find his wholeness. I have great comfort in knowing he is choosing to come back to earth. His spirit side did, in fact, tell me that he would be back on earth soon to complete some unfinished work for the good of his soul.

"Know in your heart that when you or a loved one dies,
that no one is gone."
Cameron

CHAPTER 13

Do We Ever Really Die?

Cameron

We would like to speak about heaven, hell, and purgatory. It is necessary for you to have an open mind about these subjects. We can only speak the truth from here and do not even know how to access an ability to speak an untruth. These pages are filled with truth from the soul.

What is hell? Where did that name come from? We believe it came from a misinterpretation of words in the Bible long ago. There is no hell here. When you think of the word hell, what does it bring to mind? Do you think of fire, heat, devils, torture, and damnation? What has your religion taught you about hell? Hell is only a state of mind that you create.

The word "hell" may be in your mind when you have the opportunity to review your life with the Creator. At that time, if you do not think you did what you set out to do on earth then you may put your mind into a dark state of not wishing to advance to your wholeness. You may have already mentally decided that you will be in a certain state here. When you are in that state you may decide to go to earth again with the intention of fulfilling the advancement of your soul. If there were anything like hell here, that would be it. There are no devils, no fire, nothing like that. All of that is an illusion.

Some who have come here speak of purgatory. They say it is a state in which you decide whether you are good or bad. There is no limbo purgatory state here. There is something we would like to call the lullaby state. That is when you are making a decision of whether to go to earth again, another place, or ascend to the light. That state has nothing to do with whether you've been good or bad. It is a decision between you and the Creator about where you would like to be.

Heaven probably conjures up the most beautiful things in your mind, however heaven is also a state of mind. When you come here you will feel the heavenly light pulling you deeper into its self. If you feel you have fulfilled the tasks on earth that you have set out to do, you will want to ascend deeper into the light. The light of wholeness is always a draw to us here.

There are many levels here. When we say the word "level" we do not want you to think up or down, it is not less or more. People in a state of deciding if they will go to earth because they have not fulfilled something are *no less* beautiful in spirit than those who are ready to ascend. It does not work that way here. Everyone is of the same beautiful soul. Some just have to complete more lessons but there is no difference. Decisions can be changed at any time. You may ascend to the light then decide to go to earth again, or go to many other places. Nothing is written in stone here.

Know in your heart that when you or a loved one dies, no one is gone. No one falls into a black hole. Heaven is available to anyone. The concept of the good going to heaven and the bad going to hell is incorrect. The door you call heaven is the only one open to anyone, even someone who executed the most devious acts on earth. They are harsher on themselves than the Creator would ever be. That is why it is a decision between the Creator, who is infinite love, and the person coming to our side about where they shall go and what they shall do. We hope this is a great comfort to those who have deceased loved ones to know that they don't just go away. They either ascend or go back to earth or other places.

When you or your loved ones come to our side a large greeter group is waiting. Many people who have touched your life will be waiting for you. You are never alone. All of us rejoice in your coming home. Please know that your loved ones are well taken care of when they come to our side.

You have chosen to be on earth because it can teach you so much. We realize it can very difficult, but there is much of value to learn on earth.

Often people come to our side to take care of their loved ones on earth because that's the best way they can do it. They don't feel they have the power or the strength while on earth to be of help, so they come to our side to assist in guiding their loved ones.

When you come here we take very good care of you and you take care of us. It is an exchange. We also take care of your loved ones here as they take care of us. Everything is an exchange. When you die you do not go away, for you are then truly in the light and truly alive.

Carole

Although I was baptized Catholic as an infant and went to parochial school for a few years I cannot tell you with certainty what the Catholic teachings are on reincarnation. I do remember well, though, the talk of heaven, hell, and purgatory.

At the age of six I tried to conjure up some sins so I could go to confession and receive first Holy Communion. I learned that confession was the key to communion. One highlight in our faith for me, as a young girl, was the fancy all-white dress and veil that is worn for this ceremony. I was nervous about confession and remember making up sins so that I had something to tell the priest. Venial sins were not too bad; mortal sins were the worst. I remember something in me felt funny when I had to lie and make up three sins to be able to go to first communion with my group. At six, I really did not believe I was bad or had sinned. I was confused about lying to the priest about something I didn't really do. Somehow I passed that lying off as a venial sin and hoped God would forgive me.

This experience left many unsettled questions for me. Hopefully the policy has changed in the forty plus years since my childhood. I am not a practicing Catholic today so am not apprized of the current doctrine but have heard there have been many changes.

I don't remember hearing the word "reincarnation" said out loud. It was one of those curious hushed words that was never to be asked about. As I was growing up, I had an inner knowing that when you die you don't drop into a big black hole. I thought there must be something more. Hell and devils were something I never thought existed. Purgatory, well, I was not so sure. To get to heaven I believed you must be especially good.

My awakening started with a beautiful soul called Brooke. She became ill at an untimely young age. As Brooke lay in her hospital bed in preparation for her transition to the other side, I had the honor of sitting with her many times. When we spoke she seemed to be touching both spirit and earth sides at will. An amazing calmness would come over her when she was visiting the spirit side. Often she would speak of seeing her Grandpa and others waiting, along with her cat, Gabriel, for her ascent. She passed over to the spirit side while in her early twenties.

Brooke came to "visit" me after her passing and allowed me to see her beautiful long golden bouncy curls, soft lovely face, and silhouette of her body. She even wore "wings" to let me know, for my own belief, that she truly was an angel now. But it was her eyes, those magnificent eyes that had an unbelievable depth to them, a radiance that was far beyond anything I've ever seen on earth. The complete peace, contentment, and knowing that she showed was all I needed to confirm, without a doubt, that she was truly home now, very alive and at total peace. Brooke's words confirmed that there is an extraordinary side filled with so much light waiting for all of us when it becomes our time to pass over. Bless Brooke for her guidance and gifts that she is giving to so many.

"You always have free will and the ability to make a decision at the fork in the road."
Cameron

CHAPTER 14

Who Chooses Your Path?

Cameron

People are in many different circumstances and experience many different consequences on earth. Often we hear people say, "Why me, why do I have a problem? Why do I always get the short end of the stick? What have I done to deserve this?" Have thoughts such as this crossed your mind? Could you have chosen that path, perhaps in a past life? Would that seem possible to you?

You always have free will and the ability to make a decision at the fork in the road. It's up to you, which turn you take to get to your destination. You have come to earth to complete your chosen lessons in life. The conclusion will always be the same, no matter which fork in the road you choose to take. You have chosen circumstances, in agreement with your soul, to learn these lessons well. This may have been decided upon three or four lives ago. It may be that in a previous life you didn't have the strength to learn a particular lesson. So this time you've come here on earth to try again, to seek your challenge again. Have you ever considered this concept?

Could you imagine ever asking for bad things to come your way? When bad things happen to you, it really is a lesson that you've asked for yourself. You have asked for it to be drawn into your energy. You *do* seek goodness for yourself but sometimes in seeking that goodness you have to go through a path of darkness. In that way you have challenged yourself to learn more. Have you observed that the so-called "bad things" that happen, can and do often end up being something good?

Young children often seem to be on a path of self-destruction by themselves or others. How could a young child ask for that? Our answer would be that their soul desires to learn something at a very young age. There is a merciful way that a young child innately has that enables them to forget their younger years so they may move forward with their lives and thus allows them to love as if nothing has happened.

If you see a child in a situation that you feel is undesirable, think again before you step in and change that situation. If you were to change it, the child would have to go though the learning process again in another life to learn their desired lesson. We are talking about a situation where a child is being berated or punished for something that could be talked out in a calmer and better way. Just know the child has asked for this fork in the road, perhaps not in a conscious state of mind now on earth, but in the past it *has* been asked for. This does not, of course, fall into this category if the child's life is in danger. Please take action when an adult is doing serious physical harm. When you see a situation that causes you dismay, just know the angels are watching. Your angels are always watching over you and especially the little children. Their guardian angels are totally aware when something is not in alignment or becomes too bitter or bad for the child. In this case the child will forget until the proper time of strength comes up for them to heal. We hope knowing this will lift a burden off you.

We want to touch briefly again on the homeless. They have chosen their path and are filling a debt they think they need to fulfill to add light to their soul. There is no need to feel sorry for them at all. They are just completing their mission. You may desire to look deep into their eyes and just smile. If you wish to give a coin, that's all right but is not necessary at all. They are not trying to make you feel guilty. Do not feel badly for those you see in circumstances of poverty. In many countries there are a great number of people in this state. There is no need to feel bad. That is their chosen path. To you it would seem a hardship because you are not in that space. Everyone is in exactly the situation they have designed for themselves. Since this is true does it make any sense to say, "Why me, why am I in this situation?" Just know that your soul has asked for this state but your conscious mind is not aware of that. Your conscious mind gets in and mixes it all up until your circumstances make no sense at all. Just know your heart and soul have longed for this situation and are playing it out perfectly. You are always where you should be.

Why do people become ill? There is no single answer. Whatever the reason the illness is serving a purpose. They may even bring a fatal illness into them if they wish to leave earth. That is often the way it is done to get here. That is not the way it needs to be. In the years ahead there will be a time when illness will *not* be the vehicle to our side.

If you are aware of someone who is in a state of constant illness, remember that the illness is always serving a purpose for this person. You don't need to judge it. You don't need to do anything with this, it just is. That is what they have asked for. Please be patient with people's ills and ways. Everyone is in a constant state of learning, each with their own lessons. It may become apparent to you that their path is very different than what you choose. Realize that you're only responsible for yourself and that it is not necessary to comment. When someone is ill, confined, in poverty, or in any state other than what you think they should be, the very best thing you can do is to just bless them on their path.

Carole

Long before Cameron channeled "Awakening" he said the words it contained would be healing for me and for others. He gave me a choice whether I wanted to do this project or not. The choice was always mine. I decided to go ahead, feeling that if it could in some way help other people, the time would have been well spent. Cameron offered me a part in "Awakening." I wondered what I could write to add anything of value to his wisdom.

The only credentials for me to draw from are my heart and soul. I had also done my therapy and deemed myself healed, so why do I need to write about it too? But I continued on with the adventure. I got quite a surprise as Part 1 started to unfold because by doing my story many areas were touched in my being that still needed to be addressed on a different level. By revealing so much of myself on paper, getting it out and really looking at an issue, the healing became intensely profound. I felt I was shedding layers with each chapter.

My greatest comfort so far has come in this chapter. Sometimes I have wondered how different I would have been if I had a loving, nurturing childhood. I pondered the many ways it could have been better and happier. I am now convinced I chose the path I traveled as a child and feel blessed that it turned out the way it did. I was able to forget most of my early years until I was strong enough to face the issues and heal. I was able to go along even into my forties and think all was well in those early years. I did wonder a lot about certain things, but was able to change it to a happy thought without much trouble.

Because I chose to have my hard lessons very early, life now seems to be so easy, uncomplicated and peaceful. My family and friends, who now fill my life, seem only to wish for harmony among themselves. We seem to draw strength from living a peaceful existence. What brings the most joy now is sharing feelings and thoughts. Hiding behind masks does not seem appropriate anymore. This is a very different situation than my formative years.

I believe Cameron's words have helped me to come nearly full circle in healing of my past. This comes with my forgiveness for those whom I believed had done me harm in my early years. I now understand that they were only carrying out my wishes in their own way that would teach me my asked for lessons. They did this in the best way they knew how so that I could continue my own journey to the light.

"You are all so precious and dear to us."
Cameron

CHAPTER 15

Conclusion is Ready for Now

You are all so precious and dear to us. Our hope is that many souls have opened up through the ideas and concepts in Part 1—"Awakening." This has to start at the soul level. From this day forward, if you will go through life with your fan and heart open, your journey will be wonderful, beautiful, very powerful, and far beyond your imagination.

The other part of this book will be by Rachelle. She is of a higher degree in teaching. My purpose was to create a foundation, to set the pillars down. The pillars will support future growth.

Our desire is only for your wholeness and in some measure we hope "Awakening" has assisted you in this. Please go in peace for we love each of you. Peace, be with you, always.

Cameron and Guides

"Earth is hungry for its own truth. It is my pleasure to be part of your remembrance."
Rachelle

Rachelle

Hello, my name is Rachelle. You may wonder who I am. You might wish to call me an angel, or a spirit. Whatever you wish to call me is correct for you. But actually I am you. I am your awareness.

I am all that you are, all that you stand for. I am a combination of all of you, all of me, all of my lives, all of your lives. It would be difficult for me to separate who I am, what I am, into one entity. Just as you, all is available to me. I can see all, hear all, just as you can.

My dear ones, your life on earth does not have to be so difficult. It could be fluid, easy, rhythmic. That is really what I am; I am everything that is fluid, but I'm also everything that's solid, I am rhythm. I am everything that takes up space, even the space you can't see being consumed by your air. But then you are the same.

You might wish to call where I come from "Heaven." However, heaven is a state of mind. We believe that you think of it as joy, security; you've come home. I wish to tell you now you're viewing heaven as a grain of salt. It's so much more; that is just part of it. Your vision of heaven and life is narrower than mine, not just because you are on earth but also because you have chosen to view it that way, for your perceived safety. Opening your view would allow more to be seen of what is available. You are in control of the scope of your vision.

I was on your earth so long ago, three thousand years in your time, as a girl in China. Earth has changed much since then. The appearance of the water is different and the depth has diminished, due in part, to warming trends. A balance can be achieved by earth. Nature does know how to return to its center, to what is best for her.

For now, I am observing earth, just as you have done many times.

My home is so far away. Not in your galaxy, but a great distance beyond that. It is a place of much lightness, far beyond what your galaxy has. As yet it has not been discovered and named.

I choose to be near water. My pleasure is to be part of what you might describe as one of your largest mammals. I wish to flow with them, observe them, talk to them. The closest description to what you have would be the gray whale. I flow with them in freedom and rhythm, it is joyous, and it is oneness. That is my world.

I have no boundaries. Earth creates boundaries; it narrows and constricts. I am in a place that does not confine me. I have come because many on earth have asked for guidance. I will be the voice of many who come to help you understand what you can be. Then you can forget earth boundaries, forget feeling constricted, you can be one with all, one with everything that is living.

If you were to put a form to me, the best way to describe that would be to take a broad paintbrush and just free, free your hand, let it go. This is what I am, that is what you are. Free. Free as a paintbrush. So many of you are painting your lives in dull, dark colors, the beauty you are is the beauty you can become. Before that can happen, truth must be exposed. Often earth is afraid of the truth. It would be our desire to have you be afraid of nothing and especially not self, for in that would come your freedom.

You are not alone, dear ones. We are always in your presence. You are loved, more than you can ever comprehend. We are your peace, joy, hopes, and we are your dreams. We are every goodness that you believe, that you would wish to achieve. But dear ones, so many on earth try to look for these things outside of them. They are all within you.

You are so much more than you know, so much more. Your vision on earth is no bigger than a grain of salt. For you must know, you are everything. We are you; you are us. You are everywhere, just as we are.

Often you feel powerless. But you have the power of all the heavens, the power of all the earth. You just don't know it. I have been like you. I have been on earth and understand. We view ones on earth as the most brave; it is the hardest place to be. Honor for you is great. You have traveled to earth to learn, to expand, to find who you are, and to develop love for yourself and others.

What we will be talking about in the chapters to come is not knowledge that we have beyond yours. We are in a place that does not confine us as earth does so our vision is quite clear. You know all of this. This may be a remembrance for you at some level. Fear can shut it down, and that's okay. We understand that earth has fear as its motivator most of the time. Please understand in the chapters to follow, that some subjects might offer controversy. Within that springs growth.

The excitement where we come from is that earth is changing. Earth is ready for a change. In so many different ways this is presented to you in movies, books, television, over the airways, in all the ways you have asked to remember. I speak for us only as your reminder. If you find yourself reading this book, wonderful, you are so honored; there are many, many ways to jar your remembrance and this is one. So honor yourself, right now, right in the beginning for reading this book, and for at least opening a part of your mind and heart. It is truth; it is your truth. We wish to honor all on earth, for you have asked for this awakening.

Earth is in the midst of change, as always, but the change now could be more dramatic because you're asking. We hear your desperate pleas, we do. "Help me, help me. Tell me the way." I am just one, one of many of us who have heard your pleas. In this book an open heart and an open mind would be to your advantage.

The need for this book is not for us to decide. It has been felt by so many here and so we have responded. In no way are we wishing to lecture, in no way have we come here to tell you how it must be or how it should be. We're only answering your questions; we can feel them. We hear you. Telepathically your thoughts are our thoughts. We feel it when you are scared. We feel your hurt. We hear your desperation. This book is being channeled, not from me, from all of you really, whatever your thoughts are at the time we pick them up.

We are just bouncing them right back to earth.

The people on earth have adopted their own set of rules. The planet has been having a tug of war with that. Mother Earth has a different set of rules. We wish to address that in "Emergence." We hope you will all understand that each of you, every one of you is a piece of a beautiful plan. Your freedom, your happiness; that's your ticket. Without these you narrow. Your vision and hearing shut down, and you just become. We would like to achieve in this book a oneness for all. Earth is a place where so much is learned and there is so much to teach. Everyone can do both.

The bodies you've acquired for earth are wonderful. We see some who honor their bodies, and others who do not. Most are in the latter. We say this only because even your fearful thoughts can create dysfunction or cause your body to not operate to its full capacity. Your body is a beautiful thing. Honor it. Love it. We will look into this new concept for earth.

We are going to touch upon a subject that could possibly be open for heavy discussion. It is the way you give all glory to the one called Jesus Christ. Instead, could you give yourself some glory? The higher you put him on a pedestal, the lower you push yourself down. In no way do we wish to take from you your wonderful Jesus Christ. No, not at all. We wish you to see that you can do what he did too.

The Bible came at a time when so many were searching. They needed answers. The Bible was created, partly on fact, mostly fiction. People needed something to grab onto. There was a Jesus Christ, yes, of course. Miracles yes, miracles, no. Nothing is really a miracle. You could do them yourself.

Opening your heart is what this is all about. If there were any fear in this book, it would be that you have to learn to stand on your own and not lean on a Jesus Christ. In fact, it is not necessary to lean on anyone or anything but yourself. We will explore our interpretation of what God is. God, Source, Light, please use whatever word you feel comfortable with. We shall not take that away from you. Nothing will be taken away. We don't have the power to do that. Part of what "Emergence" is doing is offering you an opportunity to open your eyes a little wider about what God represents to you.

All of you have decided be on earth at a time that offers so many decisions, so many ways to go. You are the strong ones. Strong to be on earth now. Please be so grateful for your choice.

We hear your questions; "What can I do? Why am I here? Am I powerless?" Often, others have power over you at some level. Cameron addressed this type of control in Part 1, and we shall go further with this.

Without an open soul, dear one, fear will be your leader, not love. This book is only love. There is nothing to fear. Nothing that happens in your world should create fear. We can see that the idea just presented will be hard to digest. Even what earth would call the most terrible thing that could ever happen to you would not be feared if you were based in love. To be in a state of love almost creates fear for some, though. Just for a minute, try to feel what it would be like to have no boundaries, no footing, just infinity, and be in a state of unconditional love.

If you think this is a book to tell you the future, or what other planets will do to earth, such as invasion or similar fearful things, then please put this material down. That is not what this is about. Invasion is in your mind. It is not time for you. This book is based solely on love, truth, joy, and hope. You are all those things.

We wish to address the powerful. What you presently see as power is usually fear. We hope that through reading this book you will understand power can be love. This concept shall be explored. Right now we wish to compliment you for even reading this far, because it could create fear, if you're open to it.

When you discover your own power, you will put no limits on what you can achieve, what you can do. You don't need to be on our side to achieve all your goodness, all your love, and all your wholeness. Our desire for you is to know the strength that is contained within you. Sometimes strength to ones on earth is power. True strength is love that does not proclaim fear. Fear traps you. Love releases you. Don't let your true power elude you.

All of us feel greatly honored to be a part of earth's longing for awareness, awareness for self. Earth is hungry for its own truth. It is my pleasure to be part of your remembrance. Thank you for inviting us.

PART TWO

Emergence

"The beauty of earth is like a song. If you could just listen."
Rachelle

CHAPTER 16

Earth: The Way it Is

Rachelle

Earth is alive, but not so well. She is feeling the pressure, the pressure of mankind hunting for its own awareness. Ones who inhabit earth we call the very brave. You are the ones who wish for knowledge, not only of earth, but also of self. To be on earth and to find self almost creates a maze; the two get separated. The illusion is built up of who you are almost immediately upon birth. This is where the confusion sets in. Ones who travel to earth are most honored by us because we know the difficulty of it, the challenge of it.

Earth has its natural rhythm. Most on earth don't even know it's a song. It is. The beauty of earth is like a song. Everything works together hand in hand and every bit of nature has a part. If you could just listen, listen to what she wishes for. When trees, earth, rocks and so much more are moved, transplanted, cut down, turned over for your convenience, the earth knows it. If beautiful trees are in the way, they are removed, all for your convenience, all for your view. A symphony needs all things in their proper place to create a rhythm. A rhythm that is so beautiful to your ears. Often on earth this is forgotten. An awareness of this is starting to unfold and for that she will be so grateful. Why is it that many have a conflict with Mother Earth's placement of rocks and trees? Why must you intervene? What if all was left in a natural state? Would it be unsightly? We don't think so. Maybe it wouldn't be organized enough for you. Mother Earth has her own plan, you know. Mankind does disrupt that. When this happens the rhythm is broken. The planet responds to this and starts moving, shaking, almost exploding in violence sometimes. Mother Earth is most forgiving but oftentimes the pressure becomes too much.

It's not that earth is overpopulated; it is just that the population doesn't hear the symphony going on. If you were all in sync in that, with that, it would be a very different place. First, you must be in oneness with the earth. Then, oneness with yourself and others. We are all connected. There is not one living thing on earth that is not connected. Would it be shocking to know that you might be joined to something you detest, such as insects? You're all connected. When animals, mammals, reptiles, fish, insects, everything living are rerouted, pushed away or destroyed, you're only destroying part of yourself. Nature knows exactly where to place everything.

All living things know the plan. They don't forget it like humans do. Humans know it also but they aren't aware. How could they be? Upon arriving on earth you are told to think with your heads. However, that is not where your answers really are. Your answers are deep within you. If you could listen, really listen, then you wouldn't swat a mosquito you thought was pesky. Perhaps you would understand that they too have a purpose. Their purpose is not really to bite you, not at all. Perhaps they are drawn to you as a reminder about something. We would like to get across in this chapter the importance of respecting everything that's living.

There has been much talk on earth about dramatic changes. Is this even possible? Could it happen that fast? Why must earth create such drama? Mother Earth wouldn't do that, she's very kind. Why must people think that? Why do so many not trust her? She has served you well, hasn't she? Every day you can pick up a newspaper and read about fires, floods, natural disasters or something else. Do you get angry at your planet? Then you forget, by littering, or pouring chemicals into her. This is something Mother Earth is not used to. Why must that happen? Can't humankind live without chemicals? Every scientific discovery should be looked at very deeply to see how it could create an imbalance. Money also creates a lot of friction on earth. She feels it, you know. Money has no importance to her.

Life on your planet could be very simple but you're challenging her. You are. Please put your fears aside. The earth does not want to destroy you. It doesn't. It's as if you don't trust her. If you could, if you're willing, put your fears aside. Just know the earth is very gentle. Mother Earth will do nothing to you unless you expect it. If you expect her to shake and rock and break apart, she will. She will honor you in that. Just know that she wouldn't do that of her own accord unless you expect it. She loves you so. Don't make her into a monster because she's not. Expect only goodness and that is what will happen.

When a great number of people are of one mind, one energy, all thinking in one vein, then the earth will comply with their wishes. This can be wonderful or catastrophic depending upon the thoughts. Even though you say the latter is terrible, you're still creating it by your thoughts, your fears, and by your knowing. Love your earth. Her wish is not to shake you or drop you into the sea. Please, if you could, change your thoughts. Know that this is your safety. Earth is and can be your safety. One way to remember how to do this is to spread yourself out on a beautiful green meadow, put your ear to the soil and just listen, listen to the rhythm, feel the beauty.

We know that so many tragedies happen; at least that's the appearance. Death is not a tragedy, however for the ones left behind, we understand your sorrow. Just know your loved ones who are "caught" in an earthquake, fire, flood, or other natural disasters, are so well taken care of. It was their time, dear ones. No one is caught and forced to this side. That isn't how it works. They choose to go and often many will clump together in a group and come here. Please don't blame that on Mother Earth. Know there's a reason behind everything! Earth is on your side. She's not against you. She will do whatever you wish. If you tell her that this will happen or that will happen on a certain date, she will listen and comply. That's how kind she is. She would never want to make a liar out of you, that isn't the way she works. It must start with you honoring her. Tell her she's gentle. When you honor one another your peace will come.

Carole

One of my greatest joys is to help make a connection between deceased children and their parents and siblings. One of the ways I do this is to sit at my computer and ask the young spirit if they would like to write a letter to their family. They usually respond with several typewritten pages.

A new spirit I was working with desired to write individual letters to his mom, dad and three siblings. He left earth abruptly by suicide and wanted to explain a few things to each of them. Since it seemed important to him I agreed to receive all five letters. It was three in the morning when the keys of my computer became quiet.

I was excited to be able to deliver his comforting words to each family member in the morning at his memorial service, but first I was looking forward to four and a half hours of sleep. Within seconds of climbing into my waiting bed I heard a buzzing sound by my ear. A pesky mosquito had arrived! I hid under the covers but the buzz continued to get louder. Then I remembered what Rachelle had said in this chapter about swatting even a mosquito. I was so tired and needed my sleep, how could I not swat at this pesky and noisy insect?

I decided to take Rachelle's advice and really listen. I felt silly as I asked the buzzing mosquito if it had a message for me. In response I heard, in a very clear voice, "Remember to take time for you." I waited for the insect and annoying buzz to return. This did not occur. Within the hour I drifted into a peaceful sleep.

I love connecting spirits with their grieving families. The comfort that I witness from this is so heartwarming, but I often do lose track of time and let my own needs slip. I am so thankful that my decision was to heed Rachelle's wisdom by listening to the mosquito, get my message and in turn realize my oneness with this small insect. How could I ever call them pesky or swat at them again?

"None of you are on earth by chance."
Rachelle

CHAPTER 17

Creating Your Own Spiritual Balance

Rachelle

Dear ones, we shall talk about a subject that could spur a lot of controversy. However, controversy often creates a new way of thinking, a growth. We shall discuss your Bible: what it stands for, the main player, and what is this all about? As you can tell, this chapter is not for the meek.

Who is your God? What does that mean to you? Many on earth wish to look up, up to a force stronger than them that they can lean on for security and strength.

Most on earth wish to adore someone who was on earth so long ago. You have chosen many names to adore but one of the most prevalent is your Jesus Christ. How could one man be so much to so many? He was just a man. He did have a new belief, a new way of thinking. You often feel he is your savior. We don't wish to deny that feeling "saved" is good for many. But when you fail to look at yourself, deep within yourself, for your own security or strength and look elsewhere, that creates a weakness in you.

Your Jesus has created quite a stir on earth. A great deal of money has been put into churches that you call "His house." The Son of God, you say. Who is God? What is God? Is God a strength that is stronger than your Jesus? Is God a consciousness that's come together? What does that mean to you? We do not wish to take your God from you, but ask you to look inward, into yourself. There is a great strength in there that's untapped.

If you were to meet Jesus today, he would not want all that you have done for him by putting him on a pedestal. It is the exact opposite of the message he was trying to convey. Why do you think Jesus appeared when he did? Was his message to share a new way of thinking, knowing you could all do the same as he? But the miracles you say? You could do the same. You can *all* do the same. Because you give the power to him, you don't think you could. He even said he is no different than you.

Why was he crucified? Was it because of fear? Because he was crucified, did that create guilt? Are the shrines made for him out of guilt? What if this energy was spent on knowing and celebrating self?

You on earth are so strong, so beautiful. You could be anything you want to be. You could create anything you want to create. You could do every miracle you said Jesus did. It's that belief, that inner belief, that you can really do it! You have put so much on him that you think he is the only truly special one. You also have other leaders you have named as very special. When you do that it's taking from self. All of you are so important. None of you are on earth by chance; you are to be there. You've chosen a position and a purpose.

Do you think many churches are based on fear? Do you think their constrictions are meant to keep people in line? We see many churches on earth are into control; they control through guilt. They say Jesus wants it this way or God wants it that way. You might look a little deeper into this. If Jesus were just a man like you, why would he want that? He was only love and he wanted goodness for all. The God some of you speak of is one of revenge. Therefore you must do everything the churches say or a "revengeful God" shall get you.

Must earth have leaders? Leaders to keep people in their vein of truth? What is this? Why must there be leaders in the church? What purposes do churches serve? Is it the gathering of people, the socializing, togetherness, the common bond of worship? What does the word worship mean? If you go outside of yourselves to worship someone else you're really taking from yourselves.

You have a book called the Bible. Much in the Bible has either been altered or misinterpreted. That's the sad thing. Most that has been altered is because of fear. What if you were to realize that Jesus is absolutely the same as you? What would that do? We do not wish to lessen the wonderful feelings you have for him. But please know the feelings you have for him could be the same you have for yourself. You are both in perfect alignment. You are both the same.

I speak from the heavens you say your God is from. The God you speak of is not here, only love, a community of love. Revenge is not here, there is nothing here to access that. The words "revengeful God" has been obtained for control. Here we only have love. We live for love and peace for all of you. Not one thing you do on earth shall create a situation here of revenge when you come to our side. *All* we can access is love. We only have open arms.

We only wish for you a peaceful life, a life of serenity. We're not out to get anyone, anyone who does a misdeed. Earth may tell you that, but that is not truth. Truth can only be spoken from here.

You on earth are so adored. Earth can be a difficult place: It can be confusing and seem harsh, but it doesn't have to be, it can be love. We hope in this book you will come to the conclusion that only you are in control of yourself. On earth only you should have power over you, no one else. Decisions are to be made by you about everything. If you were to be on the path that you've designed for yourself and stay on it, only goodness would be yours.

Perhaps in the larger picture you will come to recognize there is a state of consciousness so large, so huge, beyond your imagination, that is all love, pure love; unconditional love, *that* is the God that we see here.

Carole

This chapter, "Creating Your Own Spiritual Balance," would have made little sense to me years ago. I probably would have disregarded it as mainly nonsense. As I became stronger in my own convictions, the God that I used to lean on stayed firm in my mind, as a strong and stable power. The real difference was that I also became strong and found my own inner power. When this happened our distance and differences lessened until I felt little division between us.

The God/man I used to place on a throne, sitting in judgment, has evaporated. Now the God in my vision is more like a strong collection of light encompassing every living thing. To me, Jesus was a very enlightened man with a broadened way of thinking who, with his elevated ways, showed examples and guidance of inner peace.

This is a chapter that could easily be open to great debate. I know that it was a valuable part of my life to be able to lean on my old interpretation of God as a necessary part of my growth. I needed a crutch. At that time, I needed a link as well as my church's firm structure. My reality now, which is in line with Rachelle's reality, brings me an inner peace. The search outside myself is over. This long journey has enabled me to honor everyone for their own knowing and reality of their God.

"You are a beautiful energy and when you sing your own song of praise, others will come within your space singing their own song."
Rachelle

CHAPTER 18

What Are Relationships Anyway?

Rachelle

What does that title mean to you? Did you think of your relationship with others? Did you think of your relationship with yourself? What about your relationship with the universe? We are all one, there is no separation whatsoever.

On this side we are connected, as if woven, like a piece of your finest fabric. We're interlocked. There is no difference among any of us. When you come to earth the separation begins. It's as if you've been dropped on a strange planet without a road map.

As you enter school it becomes apparent that even at a very young age you are seeking someone. That's what earth says, that is what the talk is all about. You're seeking a partner. It's very subtle in the lower grades. But as you get older, this is a focus for many. Are you seeking the right person, to make you complete, to share your ideas, for companionship, to start a family? Why do you seek someone? What is it these relationships offer? Is the draw maybe to find someone to share your wonderful world with; ah what a good reason that would be. But if it's to find someone to make you complete, to find your other half, as we've heard, that would be an illusion, wouldn't it?

Often times you find someone and say, "Ah, this is the one, I shall be with this one forever." That is quite a heavy obligation to put on another person, and on yourself, don't you think? You are ever changing on earth therefore your needs and desires change with them. We find relationships as they stand on earth now really don't work very well, but everyone's seeking them. They get out of one relationship and often they seek another. The cycle goes on and on and on.

What is this thing called relationships? What is this? What if earth's custom was not only bonding with one person, but to allow bonding with many? That would go against many of your laws, wouldn't it? Earth has its own agenda of what is right, what is wrong. People often get fearful of the free thinkers.

Ones are taught at an early age what is proper and what is not in relationships. Right now we're talking about a couple that want to get married. There are many, many types of relationships to be had. Changes in relationships are happening and we see even more in the years to come. As relationships change notice that earth is seeking harmony, a flowing of other outside energies, fulfillment, and completion.

When a marriage occurs on earth it is not long before friction could take a front seat. Why must you isolate yourselves to only one other energy? That is a question to ponder, isn't it? Earth says this is the way.

We see in some countries men have many wives. That's another whole confusion, isn't it? What if ones on earth could come together only as a partnership for the time leaving commitment out of it; a partnership to seek adventure, partnership to allow children to come in, or a partnership to share love? But just know that everything is just temporary, even partnerships.

What if earth could be free and let go of any commitments? How would that be possible? Earth wishes to judge these partnerships. Everyone has an opinion it seems about what should or shouldn't happen, who you should be with. If ones on earth would realize that there is an absolute reason for being with a particular person, no matter how it appears, their judgment would subside. The relationship is not a mistake. You didn't choose wrong. You didn't; repeat, repeat,

repeat because you were stuck. You repeated the same type of relationship, because it creates a purpose as well as awareness for you.

We see many are very down on themselves when they say, "Well, here I go again in the same type of relationship." Hmm, it would be quite a different world if you would not judge yourselves on who you're with at the time. Just know this has been set up so long ago, set in motion and now it's time, time to complete it.

We see on earth that it becomes troubling when you do not allow yourself to move on, move beyond the commitment of the relationship that human rules have made. You don't allow yourself that freedom. Earth's laws prohibit many things. We look at many relationships that have been together many, many years, fifty, sixty years in your time. Commendable everyone says, "That's wonderful," and for many it is. What about the couple who have stopped their growth maybe forty years ago? What does that say? Perhaps they have not given themselves permission to grow or even realize that they can.

What if earth would allow everyone their freedom without judgment? Is earth ready for that? People judge themselves harshly. Ones on earth judge others only when they are judging themselves. They get afraid, so they must point and make comments to others. When someone feels they must judge another in a relationship, it would be best to look inward first, before making that judgment, to see if it's themselves that they are talking about.

We see the young, youth in their twenties, having a new awareness about relationships. Many of them are starting to realize who they are first, and find their purpose before entering into a serious relationship. This is accelerated growth. As each generation leaves the change is more evident. A shift is being felt.

What if right now, you were to look inward and ask yourself, "Am I as happy as I could be? Is where I am right now serving me anymore?" What would your answer be? Think of whom you relate to each day. Does that serve you? Are you ready to stretch for new growth? This is something to think about, to ponder.

Do you feel that far in the future, relationships could have a whole different meaning? There might be more than one person; there might be groups of people. What would that be like not to pair off, but to be in a group?

There is a name on earth that ones seek with diligence; they say they are hunting for their "soul mate." Other words come to mind also, but they mean the same. The search could be long and tedious. When they find their "soul mate" they know all will be well. Do you think that would be fair to label someone like that? What does "soul mate" mean to you? From our understanding, it suggests to us that there would be only one, one person for you to connect with on earth and upon uniting with them you would be everlastingly happy.

Does that sound wonderful? We would like to say that connecting with self first would create the same thing. When you meet someone and all seems perfect and in alignment, one reason for this could be that you've had many, many lives with them. If it seems magical, so be it, that is great, that is wonderful; you've found each other again. But please don't limit yourself to only that one.

Many things can happen on earth bringing new events daily. One could leave to our side, then what? On earth there are no limits, only those you put on yourself. Please be open to new ideas, new ideas about relationships. Know your happiness comes from within and not in finding someone to make you happy. We understand the special-ness of wanting to share the joy of earth with someone. But to find yourself first, that's what it's all about, and when you do, so many can bring you joy.

Earth has a curious way of making everything okay by saying, "I'll just get this. I'll just get that. I'll marry this one. I'll do that." These will bring happiness you say. However, happiness is from within. Look for a relationship with yourself first and then look outside of you. When you are complete in who you are, the knowing of who you are, the beauty of who you are, the same will draw to you. You are an energy: a beautiful energy; and when you sing your own song of praise, others will come within your space singing their own song. That, my dear ones, would be the perfect relationship. Together you would harmonize.

However, you could harmonize with many. You could do this in groups. Sure you might have a special one near you, someone to rely on if you need to. If you could start expanding your thinking process your wholeness would come to you, and you would find expanded glory with others. That, dear ones, would be the alignment ones on earth are seeking.

Carole

What a different world this would be if we were to eliminate the steadfast concept of marriage. Interesting that we continue to marry with such fervor when at least forty percent of marriages end in divorce.

I remember entering school as a small girl and finding that I thought this boy or that boy was cute. I had no idea what this was to lead to but it was a curious observation on my part. I attended an all-Catholic girls school for my junior year of high school and recall the talk and focus then was centered on boys. Having a boyfriend and going steady was the goal for most girls there. At that time, feeling I had no other options I did not look beyond love and marriage. How freeing it would have been then if I could have discovered whom I was first before seeking someone else to complete me.

Rachelle's concepts in "What Are Relationships Anyway?" certainly offers us a freedom that has yet to be explored by most people.

"Peace can never be in its truth or entirety
when there is a leader."
Rachelle

CHAPTER 19

Communities

Rachelle

What does that word "community" mean to you? That is a word that brings in many different thoughts; some you might even feel are negative. Does it mean a group of radical thinkers? Do you feel they are a group who wishes to distance themselves from others? Some groups have gone to such an extreme that they choose a leader and the leader becomes a dictator. Then the whole reason for the community is lost, isn't it? This is not the kind of community we are talking about, dear ones.

If you need to change the word to neighborhood, perhaps that would be good for you. Anything that would give you comfort would be fine. We find that words on earth have incredible power into directing your mind into thinking a certain way.

Community is the word we have chosen because it flows so well for us; it suggests an inner working by all, but our community would not be headed by a leader. Needing a leader is a vision you have created for yourself. Sometimes ones get part of the vision but something goes awry. Someone takes charge, and when that happens the others are like puppets to the one they've raised onto the stage.

The community and vision we talk about is in an area where only peace could be created. Peace can never be in its truth or entirety, when there is a leader. All of you, precious ones, are your own leaders. That's the way it must work for a true community to operate. In this place of peace, in this vision, no money need ever be exchanged. How would you live or operate? Does this sound impossible?

We believe people on earth have become so brilliant. The way to obtain everything that each person needs lies within this community. When all share their wares and talents, nothing would be longed for. How does that seem to not have money exchanged; hmm, a curious thing to think about. This community is really your world. It is. It looks so far from that now, doesn't it?

It's possible that Mother Earth has everything you need. Everything you could ever want would come from her. Do you think to achieve this earth would have to scale down a bit in its type of desires? Do you think earth has become too needy, wanting more, more, and more? This certainly would be a new way of looking at possessions. How many cars does a family really need? How many clothes? What do all your belongings represent to you? When each person realizes they are absolutely the same as another no possessions would be needed, just what you might now call staples could be necessary. The earth is capable of giving all you could ever desire to eat. Give her a chance again, but first you must un-pollute her. It seems much of your food comes from buildings! Curious.

The community vision we spoke of is far into the future. It's only a peek of what earth desires for herself and you desire for you. Somewhere all has been so misaligned. Your purpose, desires, and beliefs have been so distracted by everything manmade. It is our belief earth has almost peaked on this, and that a new awareness is awakening on earth through several different vehicles. This book is one of many.

Our love for you is so intense at this time as we see you struggle to find out who you are. We see you struggle in your isolation and with your many possessions. That is the purpose so much is being offered to your awareness in so many different ways now. We do not mean to pry into your way of life, but your burden is felt and your tears are heard loud and clear. We come in love to guide you, *only* because you have asked.

Carole

For many years I have carried a vision of a community very much like Rachelle describes in this chapter. My vision is always filled with the security of warmth, peace and belonging; along with an understanding and respect for all animals wild and domesticated. To me this community could easily go hand in hand with the multi-extended relationships she spoke of.

I often daydream how freeing it would be to have little or no possessions to care for. How wonderful to eliminate money as a way of trade since it can create heartache for so many. I would think each person would discover their own value, as they are able to share their chosen goods and trade. This way would certainly allow all people to feel equal, since everyone would be needed to fulfill their part in the community.

Not having some type of leader would really seem a challenge for our world right now. This is a very interesting concept to ponder. We would each have to find our own power and be responsible for ourselves. In this way we would not be able to judge and blame people in power for their shortcomings but would have to look to ourselves for guidance and answers. While this is a simple concept in principle it seems far from our present reality.

"A child knows no shame, they are taught this."
Rachelle

CHAPTER 20

Is Illness Only an Illusion?

Rachelle

Dear ones, today we wish to speak of something that earth has almost picked as one of its priorities. We do know, we can observe that you do not wish to feel bad. Illness is a state where the rhythm of your body signals you it needs an alignment.

When I say the word alignment, understand that you are energy and energy wishes to flow freely. When it becomes constricted, slowed down, even stopped, it will affect your well-being. How could this happen, you don't wish to stop it, we do see that. Fear is the number one culprit. So many other words could fall under fear such as; shame, guilt, etc. That is really where earth is hung up. The words that you speak have the power to create immense havoc to the human body. When fear so consumes you, shame so consumes you, along with guilt, the flow to all your beautiful parts slow down.

How can this be prevented? The states we talked about; fear, guilt, shame, and others are created outside of your body. These have come from the observation of others, who along the line have passed them down to you. Certain deeds are unacceptable on earth. If you believe that you fit into the categories earth has made; the rights and wrongs that earth has made for you, you will draw these feelings to you. Shame has to be acquired by what others tell you. A child knows no shame, they are taught this.

People feel fearful, but fear of what? Fear that they don't fit in; fear they aren't good enough to fit in? Ones on earth seek so much togetherness. They feel fear when they are not accepted and then turn inward. They ask questions like, "What is wrong with me? It must be the way I look, isn't it? Is it something I have said? Am I bright enough for this world?"

How about guilt? What is guilt? Is that something you should have done, according to others or according to yourself? Illness draws from these formable words, as you know them. You do need to feel complete, loved, and whole. All people so want to feel accepted by others.

Illness serves many purposes on earth. When people fear they do not have a position, a standing of merit, being sick can allow them some standing and can make them matter to others. We know this is not how they wish to feel; hurting, dragging, having no energy, but we see ones find that the need to be loved and noticed far outweighs the body's reaction to illness.

Illness can also allow you to leave earth. It's a way out. This is the ticket that is used most frequently. It is not time, for but a handful, to do it any other way. A day will come; a year will come, that ones will know when it is time to exit. Then people will pass over in a sleep state. That will be a time when earth has become most enlightened. But for now, it is important to try and solve this mystery of illness on earth.

Would there be any purpose in feeling shameful, guilty, fearful if you knew that you are so loved, so perfect, and your wholeness is contained as it should be? As we observe the state of humanity today we would like to have you begin to understand this concept. If you would not look outside of yourself for love, disease would become extinct.

Visualize your body as a sponge. Everything outside of it, all the outside forces, other's thoughts and all of the pointing fingers are waiting to be absorbed. The sponge soon gets saturated from all of the outside thoughts and opinions. It gets too full, too heavy, bogged down, and illness sets in. Now if you could feel your body again, as a sponge, but this time the sponge is being filled with your beautiful light, flowing in and out; just energy in and out. Every hole has to be filled with light, but with your own light. Then there would be no place for illness. How could you do this? What an impossible task, you say. Could containment of your own light become a habit? If this were so, illness would be abandoned.

Ones on earth have asked for quite a challenge. Outside influences are getting increasingly stronger, louder and brassier. How can you contain your light, your flowing? What would be the key to not allow outside influences in? Must you listen to the television and radio? And if you do listen, how can you avoid the harshness that flows through the airways? Stories with drama or brutality make the news. What would happen if you could know, really know, that earth is in heavy drama? Watch your television newsperson. Look what makes the news. In no way could we blame them. Earth is hungry for drama.

Because your lives have become so mundane you look for others to fill you up, but it never quite happens. Are you becoming tired of this? It will be a glorious day when ones can seek only themselves. There is not one thing, not one person, nor any amount of money that can fill you up to the capacity needed to keep you one hundred percent healthy. Only you can do that for you. We cannot stress enough that illness *always* comes from outside of you. You bring it into your body. You, your wholeness, your oneness with self; is your purest form of health. Then nothing would be allowed to penetrate the body sponge we spoke of.

Dear ones, as long as you are seeking your completeness and others' approval for anything, there will be illness, great illness on earth. How must it be that it could be so simple, yet so extremely difficult to listen only to self? Earth conditioning would be our answer. If you could just start pleasing yourself, then in the larger picture, you will in turn please others. When you allow others to make any decisions for you, part of your right to be who you are is shattered.

This concept is quite different than in past centuries. The teaching, "others first," was taught to the children, we understand, out of kindness to others and, to avoid selfishness; but for health in the world, that must be reversed. If you could put self first, adore self first; the glow you emit shall travel to others. It must start with self, dear ones.

The health of the world also needs attention. Mother Earth and humans are in a devastating turmoil. If you can love your earth as you love self and in turn love others, she will be as she was meant to be, a healthy and enlightened friend.

We bless all the seekers who are looking outside of themselves for their answers. However, perhaps it is time to consider the possibility of coming home to self.

Carole

This chapter addresses so much of my path in younger years. Illness was a necessary tool I used for affection. This was a sure fire way that I knew I could get attention from my family. Unfortunately it became an addictive habit in my adult years.

I'm sure my body was the perfect breeding ground for illness. Thoughts and most of my opinions were always stuffed. At that time I didn't know that memories buried alive never die, but rather, they just resurface later.

Illness really got in my way while raising my five children. It was so hard to keep up with all their needs and desires when I did not feel good myself. Often it was necessary to depend on others to watch them for my trips to the hospital. I felt badly if my operations were an inconvenience to their schedules. Being separated from my children was difficult, as my life had always revolved around them and their happiness.

Finally at forty, I came to the point when I said, "Enough." I was so tired of feeling and being sick. I began to see a real pattern to my illness and operations. My decision to let go of this way of life was not as easy as I thought. Never did I feel like a victim of illness, rather it was really who I thought I was. I was scared to think of replacing being sick with something else because I had no idea what that could possibly be. By now I was not sure of my own desires or even my identity. Life at this point was very confusing and distorted for me. Therapy was one of my keys to wellness and finding myself.

Now I know that illness resides outside of me and that I can tap into it at will by just searching outside of myself for answers and wholeness. I can now, ever so softly, feel the flow of energy inside my body. When it feels sluggish I know there is a possible issue I need to address before the flow stops, leading me straight into an illness. This flow is now in my daily awareness; as I believe it offers me freedom from hidden diseases.

Rachelle tells us that passing to the spirit side can be done without illness as the vehicle; instead it can be done in a peaceful sleep state. That sounds wonderful. I have signed up now for that way to exit, in maybe thirty years or more!

"Your pets return to you over and over."
Rachelle

CHAPTER 21

What Do Your Pets Offer You?

Rachelle

Earth has adopted a particular glory relating to their pets. We are talking about the pets that live with you, your dogs, cats, gerbils, fish, mice, and all your other special friends. What a glorious, glorious feeling it is to watch your animals become so excited as you enter the room. What unconditional love they teach you. Why do you think they are on earth? They become constant companions when you are feeling down, a little lonely, or a little scared. We find the purpose that is served by these wonderful friends is multifold. Do you feel that these constant friends are there to teach all of you in some way?

Is there anything cuter than a baby puppy or kitten when they first come into your home? They are so lively. Are they a reminder of what you are; your liveliness; your wide-open look to all around you? Where does that liveliness go? When does that become subdued? If we were to look a little deeper into that we do not believe that age in any way becomes the subduer. We believe the animals start conforming to what they see around them. People have conformed to what's around them, they have been told what is proper and what is not. The animals learn this by observing you; in one way that brings sadness. When animals are young and new to earth everything is an adventure to be had. Where did your spirit go: your spirit of adventure, of youth? Has it also conformed to earth ways?

If your precious animals were really observed, you would see yourself in them. They are one of the many gifts that have been offered to you on your planet. We have noticed that sometimes ones adopt such closeness with their animals, they almost become as one.

One thing we see that has been strived for, so many times, is trying to regain one's youth. The goal most often is to be and look younger. If you were to watch the unlimited freedom of a kitten you would see that it knows no boundaries. If you were to also act as if you did not have a care in the world, your youth could be reclaimed. But you set up too many boundaries to do that. If you could watch how animals play and relate to each other you would learn a lot. Is it only you that gives them restrictions; how could that relate to giving yourselves restrictions? Your animals are there as your constant reminder of the joy in yourself. They are an extension of who you are and they travel with you constantly.

Your pets return to you over and over and over. Prior to this life together there has been a commitment, a bond between you and your animals. They are there to help you understand, reason, and reflect your actions back to you. A greater awareness to this way of thinking about pets is becoming more prevalent. The animals we speak of love their duty and service to you. Have you ever noticed that frequently a very sweet, content, and loving pet changes direction and becomes evasive, scared, and might even bite you and others? What would this suggest? It's not that your pet has turned on you; perhaps the real message is you have turned on yourself.

Pets are very grateful to be in the position of guiding you. To guide you fully it requires your observation and ability to listen to them. We see harshness can come over some people, especially with the canine species. A harsh owner will turn on a dog and even destroy them. If one would only realize that in doing this, self is also being destroyed, perhaps an awareness of this would bring more caution. Your animals offer only unconditional love to you; that love helps guide you through what sometimes would appear to be a dark maze on earth.

This brings up the subject of what can you do for your animals that are hurting. Hurting to such a degree that it becomes most apparent their time has come to leave their body. We see people becoming very distraught when they must make this decision for their pets. They ask themselves, "Should I help them leave or should I not?" If you are observing your beloved pet in such a state, may I suggest that you treat them and their illness, exactly as you would like to be treated at the end of your present life term. Would you find it comforting to have gentle help in leaving your body or wouldn't you?

If you couldn't get an answer that you are satisfied with by putting yourself in your animal's position, perhaps you could ask them. Does it seem strange you would get an answer? We do believe that many on earth know for a fact they can communicate with their animals. It is a knowing of how their pets are feeling that becomes a part of them. The answer is felt within them. This takes a bit of trust because your pets do not open their mouths and words, as you understand them, do not tumble out. Give your animals a chance, let them speak, communicate, and share with you what they observe about you. They are there to serve you; but not in a way that you need to feel superior to them at all. They are serving you with love. Can you not do the same for them?

We see billions of dollars are spent in putting these wonderful friends in luxury. That is commendable on earth. Earth says that shows love. The only comment we wish to make on this is that a hug, pet, scratch, walk, or anything that allows them to be in your energy is worth so much more to them than what the stores can offer. They are only there to be accepted by you. Their message is: for *you* to be accepted by *you*.

You live in a fine world and animals are a great part of it. As you allow your awareness to expand to these household friends perhaps that awareness will travel beyond, to all living things. We would love to expand on the animals outside your home at a later date. This will help you understand that every living thing on earth is connected to you as surely as your pets are. Enjoy these pet friends. When you give them special hugs know that you're hugging yourself as well. In this way you will find the glory of you.

Carole

To have Rachelle confirm something that I have often thought and wondered about is very comforting. Knowing that my animals will return to me over and over just might make it a little more bearable when their time to leave does come. My overwhelming sadness when a true fur friend leaves makes me cautious to replace them with another. To repeat this cycle with a new small creature of unconditional love just seems too much. Now, however, with this confirmed knowledge, it seems different.

Animals often clearly communicate with me. They are straightforward and seem to disregard any filtering of their words as most humans do. They come forward with their messages, much like a very young child, without any reservations. I deliver these messages to their owners if asked, otherwise I just listen to their absolute clarity and wonder what it would be like if we were all so forthright in our speaking.

My joy work has always been with people, rather than animals. When the animals started to talk to me I really did not think too much about it. Although my heart is so touched when they come forward and offer me their statement to confirm or clear up a notion I have had while preparing to give their owners a reading. I am always amazed at how they are so very aware of their people's happenings.

Rachelle stated that our animals mirror us and constantly offer messages. I realized that this meant my own animals are mirroring me and are also trying to speak. I started to listen to them at home and learned a lot about why they portrayed certain behaviors. Sometimes home is just too close and familiar to properly notice what is always occurring. The animals are often in a flurry of greetings and always looking for their share of attention. When I took the time to really listen I found my furry friends had many priceless messages for me.

*"We believe there is a desire on earth to be able to give yourselves
permission to just be, without guilt."*
Rachelle

CHAPTER 22

Self in Its Purest Form is Truth

Rachelle

What are you? Who are you? Why have you chosen to be on
earth? Do you know your purpose, your path, or your destination?
Do you have a conclusion on earth? Ones who just seek your planet
as their playground or as their school become so heavily disillusioned.
Why would we use the word playground in conjunction with the
word school or teachings? Could they possibly be the same? We do
not speak of the formal schools that people have created for
themselves. We are talking about the school that creates experiences
such as: understanding, joy, peace, satisfaction; all the experiences
that earth has to offer you; the experience of life on earth.

Joy is the number one offering that Mother Earth can give to you.
Your days become so busy, hectic, scattered and serious that you
forget it offers any joy at all. What is all the rush? What is all the
scurrying accomplishing? Why all the deadlines you put on
yourselves? If you don't make a particular time frame, how big would
the crisis be? Do you put those restrictions on yourselves and others?
Do you criticize ones who don't conform to specific deadlines, certain
rules of time? Does it not take the joy away when you become so
rigid with yourself and others that you give no leeway?

How could an earth operate without time? Earth relies on the
clock second only to money. Would it be curious to you that we
operate here with neither one? All is in uniform, perfect alignment

and it is all in proper timing. There is not urgency at all where I am; it is a knowing that all will be accomplished, as it should be.

We watch young mothers and young business men hurry scurry to such a degree that the children involved with these families are rousted constantly from their playtime, from their dreamtime. But if this were ever to see a change, how would you stop it? How would you stop the treadmill? What would happen if all of you were to take a day off, just for yourselves?

Would you think everything would crumble around you if the grocery stores, malls, and service stations were not in operation? Have you become so dependent upon others for your entertainment that you don't know how to do it for yourselves? If any time is left over we often see ones almost mesmerized by television or by hand held games. Does that type of activity really denote who you are? When things become calm and there is no entertainment from the mall, television, or other distractions, we often observe that people become bored and look for a form of entertainment.

We believe there is a desire on earth to be able to give yourselves permission, to just be, without guilt. When would it ever be possible? What generation is going to take the first step and feel it is absolutely not imperative to have their children step on the treadmill with them? How many activities do you need to involve them in, introducing them to this way of life? We become sad to observe that parents sometimes find it necessary to boast of their children's many diverse achievements and accomplishments. Would you do that because you do not feel fulfilled yourself? Again we don't wish to pry into your way of life but seeing ones so scattered on earth, trying to keep up with the next one, is disturbing to watch.

You ask for a slower way of life but who is willing to step off that treadmill? We see a few have already done this. Can you allow others to just be? Even allow the words: lazy, unproductive, and unmotivated, not to slip into your vocabulary? Each person is on earth for a reason. Their purpose is quite defined to them, even if their conscious mind is not aware of it. What they are doing and achieving, no matter how it looks to you, is what they need for their own projected growth on earth.

Nature offers an array of things to observe that could keep you busy every moment of your day. Observing and listening to the beauty is almost impossible on the treadmill we spoke of. If you step off you will realize you are so much more than the hurry-scurry and the commitments. You are there for you and no one else.

Others do come into play and into your space to share the joy of earth, and to share your joy of you. That would be the ideal. You are the same as nature. You are the beauty, you are the stillness; you are part of the symphony that is going on constantly. It would be our greatest pleasure if at sometime you would allow yourself to be only you, the quiet of you. Listen deeply within yourself to the beauty that awaits your discovery. You need to go nowhere for this, just gather who you are and look within.

Whether you are on the treadmill or not we wish to conclude this chapter with our unwavering, unconditional love for you.

Carole

How I wish I could have had the knowledge of this chapter while raising my children. If I had, our lives could have been a lot less hectic and much more peaceful. In this chapter Rachelle offers all of us simple life-changing wisdom.

I remember listening to other parents as they talked about this class or that sport their young ones were part of. I felt guilty, thinking they were showing more love to their children than I showed mine, since they had them involved in so many activities. My distorted thinking then was that I must also get my own four young children, all under eight years of age, involved in many things too. This was quite a feat to get all of them to their respective places without one of them getting tired and crying to go home. If even one of the classes ran over ten minutes it would throw the whole day's schedule off and someone would be late for his or her destination.

We played this ridiculous game for years. I'm not sure the children even enjoyed the classes and somewhere I lost more of myself in this constant whirlwind. I often wish I had those years back with them so we could just stay home together with no pending schedule looming over our heads.

There is twenty years' difference between my first and last child. I entered my last child into school while I was in my mid-forties and carried with me a whole new attitude. The choices for youth activities seemed to have doubled in the last several years. But this time I let our little boy map his own pace and path. He made good choices for himself. He eventually zeroed in on soccer, remained with it throughout high school and to the present day.

It is my belief that this child benefitted by not constantly being rousted from his play, in his early years, to meet a fixed schedule. The most evident thing I observed was that he has always been able to entertain himself for long periods of time; neither wanting nor needing, any outside stimuli.

I often wonder if I may have robbed my older children from knowing a part of themselves, by trying to entertain them constantly with outside activities, primarily chosen by me, in their younger years. I will never know the answer, and will not hang any guilt on myself. I was so unaware how to mother and nurture my little ones. I let my love for them, and others' ways, guide me. Rachelle's offerings on this subject makes such sense to me; and most surely allows the child and adult a concrete start to their own path.

"Your body will tell you what it likes to eat, what it doesn't if you listen, really listen."
Rachelle

CHAPTER 23

Alignment With Self is Possible

Rachelle

When you chose to come to earth a body was a necessary vehicle to become one of its inhabitants. What can it matter how a body looks if it is only the vehicle to sustain yourself on earth? But being so visible, it is often on stage for judging by yourself and others. People direct so much of their energies to their bodies. Often what you copy from others, or experiences you have, do great harm to bodies. This comes in the form of illness, aches, pains, and even death. Why are you so consumed with the body? We feel the body is of the least importance to who you are, to what you stand for.

We see no body, only the true of you, the light of you, and the soul of you. If everyone were to be stripped of their bodies then everyone would look the same, then what? Would judgment then have to be put aside? That's a curious thought. We wish to say all bodies are beautiful, because you're all beautiful in choosing them. Your body is perfection for you.

What if you were born and were not the perfect standard that earth has set up? How would you fit in? How would you compensate for your perceived lack of physical perfection? If you were the only person on earth, whom would you compare yourself to? The word "compare" wouldn't even be in your vocabulary. You would be perfect, wouldn't you? If you could think of yourself in that way, without comparing, you would be assuring yourself you are perfect.

Earth has adopted models of what you should look like; how tall you should be, what you should weigh, how you should look, even to the color of skin you should have. Earth has certain ideas about what is best and what is not. We see a lot of magazines and books that tell you what is the latest way to drape your body with the highest fashion in clothes. We do understand how your world operates; we have all been there. If your souls could be adorned and draped as people do their bodies, possibly it would do some good.

Food plays a great part in how the body feels. May we suggest you could be content with yourself just by listening and feeling what your body is telling you? A very simple way to keep your body in alignment would be for you to ask yourself how you feel; "Do I feel good today?" In this way you would be in tune with your body's needs, telling you what it likes to eat and what it doesn't, if you listen, really listen. Often your body reacts violently to certain things you put into it.

Drugs also play a great part in how your body feels. It appears many drugs, over the counter or otherwise, are given to combat what non-foods have done to your body. A lot of illnesses also stem from additives, preservatives, fillers, etc. It seems mandatory for your wholeness that you get out of this cycle.

Life on earth today has become so fast-paced that eating on the run seems to be the chosen way. Your digestion is really on the run too. As you begin to believe you are worthy of feeling good, you may allow more time for yourself in the eating department. Your body is asking for fuel, but give it time, dear ones, to savor every bite, to do its work.

We have noticed that much of your fuel can hardly be identified. Do you think your body might have the same problem? Earth has come such a long way and we wish to compliment you on that. You can pick up most foods and see every ingredient. That is a start. What if you were to have your food come straight out of the garden? Pure fuel. No side panels to read about what's in there. As you learn to love and nurture yourself in a way that feels good to you, your body will respond.

We see that illness comes from many sources now on earth. Many things can create an illness in the body. One of the newer ways to this is; products put in food that really have no place in a body. These products do not come from the ground or the trees, they're manufactured. We do not wish to take the joy of your handy foods away from you but we notice that an awareness is occurring on earth about what is in your cereal boxes, packaged mixes, and other foods. Perhaps this may open even more of an awareness to read further down the panel to see what you are really eating.

You have so much quick food at your fingertips. We see your world has become so busy, so active that the family dinner table is hardly used. We wonder how fast it will get, how busy, how congested, before it is realized that you have a choice. How could you slow down? How is that possible with so much happening at one time on earth? Nurture your lovely body with foods that leave you feeling good, with no repercussions, no antacids to take; one way to change this might be to allow yourself time to just be.

Earth is to be enjoyed, savored. Each moment cannot be totally fulfilled, totally felt, when the fast pace pushes you through one day into the next. Perhaps every so often you could eat something that makes your body feel good, saying to yourself, "I'm going to allow this time for me because I am perfect and I deserve it." If once in awhile you would allow that, the benefits would be tenfold, to the benefits from the busyness of your life.

We love each of you, it doesn't matter to us your gender, color, height or size; you are perfection just as you are. Someday you could give yourself the gift of knowing you are perfect. Also give yourself the gift of time, and the gift of feeling good when you get up from the table. That, dear ones, would be the true honoring of self.

Carole

Sometimes it is embarrassing for me to read what Rachelle has channeled. It feels like she is talking straight to me and I wonder how she knew exactly what had plagued me for years. Ah, yes, the body. It was my constant reminder that I was not of "perfect" height or weight.

I quit wishing to be taller than my 5'4" by the time I finished high school. But the weight was there every morning without fail; as I thought of what clothes I could fit into ran through my head. The results would pretty much set the tone for the rest of the day. I would partake in breakfast if I felt okay about myself, otherwise I would not eat until two o'clock. By then I was quite hungry and would stuff down anything available, mostly sweets or breads. This pattern continued for many years.

The thought of listening to my body would have sounded absurd then. I had adopted the pattern of grabbing anything packaged to fill my need for an instant snack. My body finally did react to my poor, erratic eating behaviors. It started to give me loud undeniable messages through stomach-aches, and over acidity with prolonged heartburn and constant tiredness.

I decided to try to reclaim the health and energy of my youth through my food. I started eating more fresh fruits and vegetables. I tried to avoid most packaged goods. I started asking my body what it would like to eat. I was not surprised that the feeling I usually got was that something fresh and crisp was desired.

I have listened to the feelings for my body's needs for several years. I know that if I take a bite of what my eyes want and ignore what my body wants, heartburn will always get the last word. I no longer consider that I am my body but rather that it is just a necessary attachment for me to nourish. In this way the health and energy of my youth has been reclaimed!

"Finding the source of who you are, the joy of who you are takes some inner digging."
Rachelle

CHAPTER 24

Being Self-Assured is Your Source of Joy

Rachelle

You are one that is so special. No one else is like you. Much like a snowflake; all are different but combined together you all become an intense beauty that spreads upon the earth.

Finding the source of who you are, the joy of who you are takes some inner digging. We can see your beauty and tell you how wonderful you are. But why would you believe us if it does not feel that way to you? When we observe all of you we see everyone as different yet the same. That may sound confusing, however, each one of you is a part to a puzzle on earth and without each part the puzzle could not be complete. So your footing on earth is absolutely imperative to create the whole picture of who earth is, as a people.

If you were to look into yourself a little deeper would that present a fear to you? If it does, perhaps something is hiding. Fear has a way of stopping you from looking deeper into yourself when the time is not right. No one could push you into your search of self unless you are ready. No amount of belittling, shame from others or saying "You absolutely must do it" would have any long-term effects.

The perfect time to look into self is known only by you. If you see others around you discovering who they are, you might listen to know if this is your time to look within. Feel if fear is preventing this. There is not a right time; there is not a wrong time to try to discover self. We will tell you that when your fear fades, if even for a moment, perhaps that opportunity might just be opening up for you.

Often the fears you harbor inside have been placed there long ago. Sometimes the unknown fear becomes so large, so great that it is pushed down below conscious awareness. This creates an illusionary state. Fear has a way of accentuating, building up, ballooning beyond all proportions to what is fact. It shall be a time of great discovery for you when your desired time comes to seek who you are.

We see you as being able to recognize that there is more to who you are, to who you can become, than meets the eye. The feeling you occasionally get of how great you could be and what you can achieve is limited. Actually you're feeling only a small percentage of what the truth is. You have been on this side many times, the remembrance of that, the feeling of that is merely being uncovered as you discover you.

Earth does not have to be harsh or even a mystery. You can be in full awareness of everything going on around you. At this point on earth however, you would be among a small minority. We truly do understand the comfort offered by waiting to uncover yourself with the masses. We would like to achieve in this chapter a greater awareness of what you are. A self so much larger than who you think you are is now waiting for you just beyond the horizon. It's there and it is also here.

Our vision is not tunneled, like it is on earth to see the truth of you. We can see beyond the horizon. So allow us to bask in your greatness; that would be our pleasure. Just know that you are capable of so much more than you presently believe. The truth of who you are is just within an arm's reach; it is there waiting. There is no time frame. When you are ready you shall know and achieve your greatness.

Carole

Life for me now is full and blissful. That statement would have been impossible for me to write before and totally untrue just a few years ago. I was into my mid-forties before I had any desire to really address some nagging thoughts and reoccurring scenes.

I stepped into therapy without fear. I had a few issues I wanted to address but I had no idea that they stemmed from other deeply hidden past events. This connection made sense, though, when I was able to connect all the puzzle pieces of my life together. Stopping my progress while in session crossed my mind several times for I was not sure what discovery might be connected to my nagging unsettlement. The bits and pieces of some scenes have always been in my awareness, but never complete enough for me to grasp a full picture. I used to cancel an appointment, only to rebook it again within minutes. Some days I would just drag myself to the therapist's office with the intent of saying nothing, but something inside always changed that by mid-session.

After years of therapy and healing I found it took about the same length of time to get my life sorted out and settled with my new knowledge and intentions. I shutter to think where I would be today had I not decided to seek help. I was drowning and the therapists were there with the life rings. I can now swim on my own, and life is great!

"Whatever you choose in this life to become is perfection and should be held up by no one in judgment."
Rachelle

CHAPTER 25

Fear of Self is Your Real Enemy

Rachelle

Dear ones, we observe that many of you wish to escape from yourselves. If you knew who you really are we do not believe this would be so. Your mind has created an untruthful illusion of yourself. What are you afraid of? Are you afraid of others digging deeper and finding out whom you really are? Even that last sentence may create a scare in some.

The mind begins digging up who you are from the dark depths of memories that have long been forgotten. You are so complex; the child within you, who has endured un-pleasantries, sees experiences differently than the adult you. The child's experiences become exaggerated and loom much larger than they really are. This is caused by fear. Fear of what you might find goes completely off the scale.

So many times memories you don't wish to allow up yet, are often not nearly as intimidating as what put them down there. When children experience a time in their life that might create a fright they have a way of setting it aside to be looked at later. The problem with setting it aside in a child's mind is that it becomes so distorted, so big, so huge. Perhaps all your life you might be running from something that really wasn't there at all. Just know that children often fantasize and the fantasy becomes part of the scene. It takes clear uncovering to find the truth. Your feelings are your key to knowing if this was real for you at some time.

We are pleased to observe that so many of you are seeking to uncover your past through your inner child. We borrow the words "inner child" from earth's vocabulary. We see many are overly dependent on their therapist. Such a dependency creates a burden and weakness in you. While it is wonderful to have proficient therapists helping you discover you we find the best are those that teach you how to find your own way after their healing service is done. It is your job to take care of yourself. Relying on anyone else for your answers weakens all.

Would it surprise you to learn that it does not matter if you accomplish anything on earth? Achieving in the earth sense—fame, position, acclaim—does not make a difference in who you are. When you observe someone in a so-called state of "weakness," there is no way for you to know, or for us to know, what they are achieving by this state. We can observe and tell you what it appears they are doing and what the conclusion might be. But only they, by their choice of free will could change that in an instant. Only you dear ones have your answers.

You came to planet earth with enough strength to do anything it offers you. It is only yourself and others who limit you. Upon arriving on earth there is not one person with any more strength than anyone else. Whatever you choose to become in this life is perfection and should be held up by no one in judgment, lest to judge themselves. Peace be with you.

Carole

The inner child concept was introduced to me in therapy. At first I was a bit skeptical. My thinking was that small children really do not remember anything from the past, so how could they be involved? I was absolutely shocked to witness the vital role my inner child had in my healing.

Small children speak from such a clear path of truth without any reservations. I soon became the observer to my own trauma as my inner child replayed my past. What was most amazing is how I could detach my adult self from the scene I was viewing; yet child and adult were the recipients of the healing. It became apparent that my inner child had been running my daily life for years. An adult can become upset or react to something for no apparent reason. It is the child deep within who holds the keys to the understanding of why an upset or reaction was happening. Until the "why" is explored the upset or reaction normally continues each time it is triggered with the same stimuli as before. Now that my inner child has been listened to, addressed, calmed down and is happy, I the adult am in charge.

During an intuitive reading I find that the inner child of the person sitting across from me will often speak when their adult self holds back. This is fascinating to watch. Children in their truth have a way of getting to the core of most problems much faster than the adult. The inner child holds onto secrets of the past that their adult has long ago stuffed and forgotten about. The child has them safely stored away, deep within the person until enough strength is gathered to take a deeper look.

It is my belief that without the help of my inner child I would still be undergoing therapy and desperately trying to unravel my gnawing pangs of discontent.

"You are many places at once."
Rachelle

CHAPTER 26

Within Hardships Springs Growth

Rachelle

We would like to address the pain that people seem to inflict on others. Pain can be created through circumstances, illnesses and even the presence of others around them that they do not desire. Goodness, why must people create such harshness sometimes? What purpose could this possibly serve? As we view your faces we see more frowns than joy. Is it possible you have chosen to create such disharmony for yourself?

Upon our observation of the world would you believe that out of all the dark places spring light, even lighter than before? The experiences on earth can be viewed as either joy or hardship. How could it be possible that people could experience the same circumstances but have different conclusions? Some create joy, a knowing and better understanding, yet others create bitterness, hardships and become victims. How can it appear so different? The answer may sound simple. If you were to view each event you step into with love and an open mind your conclusion would most likely be an enhancement of your knowing.

When you are caught up in fear the whole dance changes. Besides experiencing the pain this causes, it also leaves the body with a residue. Your body in turn must do something with this. It may hide fear away in a long forgotten pocket to be brought up again at a time when you might be feeling particularly low. This pocket becomes a target and a magnet for other small ills to collect. Very soon it grows and a monster is created in your body.

Pick a disease, any disease; many names can be applied here. Whatever disease, whatever hurt you believe you can handle will be experienced in that pocket. We see cancer as one of the favorite ones. Cancer has high drama. It reflects to humans that the body is giving up. When a cure is found for all cancers, other illnesses will be created. The body feels all of earth's drama; your body shall reflect it if you choose to become a participant.

How can humans guard themselves against such things? Are you victims? You don't have to be. While the consciousness of people at this time makes it difficult to prevent or overcome illnesses, know that it is possible. Does this just happen to people? How could you assure yourself you would not fall prey to these many diseases? It is when you can come to the center of yourself knowing your purity, goodness and knowing absolutely that disease will not be in your body. There are more reasons people choose to carry on the drama of illness than we can list here.

We observe you are so much more than can be observed by you on earth. You are many places at once. We see that because our vision is not narrowed, nor was yours when you were on our side. Many reasons illness has become so prevalent on earth is that you deny the many good parts of you that you do not yet have a full awareness of. Until you believe the all of you does exist, illness will not cease. To benefit the part of you which inhabits earth would be a wonderful start. The first thing you must know for disease to cease is to realize that you are not at ease with yourself now. If you can step into the awareness of the all of you, the beauty of you, then disease could not possibly be in your energy.

Look inward, dear friends, and see your beauty, see your perfection. Concentrate on that, because you truly are viewing perfection. Forget what outside sources say, your truth is in knowing your perfection is self-contained inside of your skin, not outside. A wonderful start to who you are would be to turn your light up and let it glow. We love you so.

Carole

Fear had control of me throughout a substantial part of my life. I probably would not have identified it as such, as it was a shrouded fear. I always wanted to have others like me and this became an important desire of my youth. In school my own identity was easily lost in a crowd of children. My attention would often center on someone I thought was liked and received notice from others. My security then was to try to be and act like them.

In a few years I settled on being a "yes" person. Somewhere in that mode I lost track of what my own likes and dislikes were. This seemed a lot better, though, than facing the fear of not belonging. As an adult, in my search for self, people offered the suggestion that if I would learn to love myself then all would be okay. But how do you love yourself if you have no idea who you are? The fear of finding out who I was or was not put that discovery on hold for a decade.

Learning to love myself and like who I am just naturally unfolded with and beyond my years of therapy. It was a slow process for me to regain trust in who I really was and learn what that meant to me. To be able to identify myself with conviction offers me a boundless freedom I would not have thought possible before.

"All of you come to earth with an instinct to preserve your body in a healthy state until your desired job is done."
Rachelle

CHAPTER 27

Within Your Consciousness is Your Real Reality

Rachelle

Does this title create confusion for you? Do consciousness and reality mean the same thing to you? Does the real of you exist in your conscious mind? If we were to say "yes," would your answer be "It could not possibly be because I don't know everything."

The adventure of who you are is right before you. Your truth of who you are, who you really are, is always right on the tip of your tongue. The thoughts in your conscious mind can be cleared to find the reality of you. You have to dig for your truth one layer at a time.

Earth offers you a way of creating a balance between head and heart. It is found in that little voice, that little nudge and a knowing that stems from the heart. Your first thought, your first inkling may be "Where does that come from?" But it takes the head to allow it to be voiced within you. The combination of the two is your reality. It's being able to discern which is truth and which is not.

Heads may seem to have gotten a bad reputation from us; let's look a little further into this. Heads do play a great service on earth of course. You need the cells in your brain to be alive and think. As you think you also have the backup of your feelings to consider. Both are valid. It is just that your heads have become so cluttered with what others tell you and what others think of you that it feels more important than your own truth. Stop and ponder if some words belong to you or have you adopted them as your truism because of something someone has told you?

Hearts hold information also; however, the heart can hold only love. Be assured that the feeling part of you is always truth. The head part of you can be the same; however, your head can hold love and fear. If you could discern in your mind between the two, think how much more powerful you could become to who you are. Being able to use both would be the wholeness of you.

We see many on earth who wish to only follow their hearts; that is a start, and is wonderful to watch. Because earth has so many choices a head is also necessary. If the head and heart can come into alignment it would be beautiful. Heads do store much fear. Sometimes fear can be a motivator. You might wish to see if in your head you could switch to love as your motivator.

You may say, "I must put fear in my small child about running into the streets, because a car may come right in their path and then what?" If a child was taught love, love for self, perhaps they would figure that out and not run into the street. Of course it is necessary to caution children as they are growing up but put no fear in it, dear ones. A child could be raised with no fear at all and be perfectly safe in your world. All of you come to earth with an instinct to preserve your body in a healthy state until your desired job is done.

Think of the fears you were taught as a child, do you think any of those have served you well? Parents have cautioned their children so much about other people that they blindly go into their life with a preconceived notion about their safety. What are adults so afraid of? Why do you feel children are so helpless? If children are viewed as helpless they will only grow into helpless adults and in turn further the cycle. Do not cripple your fine children and world this way. Each new soul who arrives on earth has the capability and the strength to stand on their own. You must believe that.

Think of your Jesus Christ; do you believe he was coddled? Or do you believe people stood back in awe of him, trusting he knew his own way? Trust your children and know they came with that same strength. If a small seed could be planted in that direction then we have achieved in this chapter what earth is really seeking for its future generations.

Carole

It took several years of being satisfied with myself before I was able to allow my feelings to become my primary guide. I was taught that my knowledge and answers resided in my head. The little nudges from within I ignored. The inner messages that I could hear and feel were given little credence by me.

I was slow to put my hand up in school to answer questions asked by the teacher. I easily remember my confusion when I would hear or know the correct answer from within but would be too cautious to speak, because I didn't know it in my head. School would have been less confusing had I given more validity to my inner knowing.

Creating a balance between my head and my heart became a little tricky. The heart was actually the easiest for me to follow but I quickly realized the head had to also become important if I were to remain a stable part of our society.

To allow our children the freedom from fear as Rachelle suggests, could transform our world into ways that have not yet been imagined. Unfortunately as the parent I thought it was my duty to warn my little ones about this or that happening. And of course I was only drawing my information from my own past experiences and was also relaying what I had heard over the years. I will not hang back and feel guilty for any of my past warnings but will move forward with this new awareness.

"Children have a way of knowing what is real and what is not."
Rachelle

CHAPTER 28

Confusion of Self Often Begins in Childhood

Rachelle

Who are you? How do you become so detached from who you really are? Upon arriving on your great planet you are free of boundaries, corners or judgments; only free will is yours. Earth has adopted a way to strip most of that from you upon arrival.

Is it possible that even the tiniest infant could take care of its own survival? To understand this, the observation of baby animals and insects would be helpful. The caring of a human infant becomes a huge obligation to the mother and father. The parents set up a more difficult job of raising a child than is really necessary; we are now talking about all the things that are given to the child to make them comfortable. We are not talking about love, holding, caressing or the feeling of safety parents give to their children. We are talking about what is bought in the stores to be sure every whim and desire is granted. Excessive buying can even occur for items now thought necessary for the child's survival.

How is it possible that so many generations ago children were just as happy without television, hand-held games and the many places of entertainment available to them now? Some parents we see have opted for a simpler life for their children. Upon giving less to them, more will actually be achieved in the long run.

Do you buy children gifts out of guilt? We observe many show their love through gifts. Many feel that because their time is so limited that this will let the children know how loved they truly are. Children have a way of knowing what is real and what is not. Five minutes spent with them, with your full attention directed their way, would mean more in the larger picture to these small ones than the newest game on the market.

A cycle has become apparent that is very hard to break. It happens when children say, "Well, my friend has one of those, why can't I have one?" And of course to show your love you comply. Earth would be quite a different place if all adults could be in a state where money was less important than the child.

Many mothers are unable to stay home with their children. Out of necessity, daycare centers, sitters, and schools for the very young have become a big business. Could we plant a small seed and ask you to look back into the ways entertainment for children was done long ago, before it became so large? Earth passes children by when they gaze, hour after hour, at a television or at a hand-held game. A walk in the woods, park or any area close by that is not heavily populated could be a nice distraction sometimes. Earth is so beautiful, so big and is waiting for you.

Children appear happiest to us when they are part of the community. This would not be so when they stare endlessly at a television that demonstrates so much violence. The world that they watch could become theirs without proper guidance.

We are pleased to see many on earth have put away the need to achieve, achieve. Money no longer becomes their draw. If you ever were to take a trip to countries where poverty is mainly the way, notice the children. Their happiness seems to come from within. They are not searching outward for any form of entertainment. Just to connect with you is enough joy for their day.

We love all of you so much. The little children become disillusioned and confused with so many schedules and choices of what to do next. New toys appear to be losing their luster faster and faster. It would be a delight if adults could have these little ones look within and discover whom they are and what they can achieve, without so much outside entertainment. You are all so powerful on earth, the power of self-containment and self-entertainment is right at your fingertips. Money does not have to be involved at all.

Perhaps you could teach your little ones the joy of discovering who they are. Then when they grow into adults there will be no question, they will know exactly what they wish to do with their lives. It would not be lost in a maze of confusion as it often is now.

Carole

Buying gifts or excessive possessions for children seems so wrapped up with our love for them that it may be hard to break the cycle. I am now more financially free to buy for my grandchildren and find the temptation to do this now could easily be magnified with so many new and advertised toys and gadgets on the market. I wonder now, though, how many times I fell into the trap of guilt when buying for my own children.

My four older children were raised without ever sitting in a car seat, wearing disposal diapers, using spill proof cups, having a baby monitor in their bedroom or playing with most of the plastic toys that are now available. Years later, when our last child was born we were told we could not take him home from the hospital without putting him in a proper infant car seat. We had to buy several more to fit his increasing weight before he could sit on the seat like the rest of us. When did this fear creep in? I realize we have more and faster cars on the road. But it feels like fear to me.

I got caught up in all the new gadgets to make this last child safe and comfortable and, I reasoned, happy. It would have been too hard for me to ignore all the new products available. Even choosing a stroller was a mind-boggling task; so many different types and some with its own specialty for a particular type of outing.

A trip to Egypt a few years ago convinced me that children could be just as happy without all the excess we surround them with. We were told back home that the school children love retractable pens, so I took several along. The youngsters were delighted to be handed these but it created fighting among them. The children who had the dirt as their playground and nothing but a rock and stick seemed content and happy. They loved to watch tourists and would give me a long smile when our eyes met.

We had a layover at Kennedy airport on our trek home. It was a rude awakening to hear a crying child. She was demanding something and she wanted it right now! I realized it had been three weeks since I had heard a child whine or cry for anything.

I have great honor for parents who are able to stop this cycle of excess that we have created. I was not strong enough in my own self worth and convictions to be able to cease this with my own children. Today it seems that so many new parents have an enlightened view to the pitfalls of too many material trappings. As more adopt this way I believe the future will hold happier and more centered children.

"Look within, discover who you are."
Rachelle

CHAPTER 29

Discussion Within You is Your Reality

Rachelle

How would you describe yourself? Who are you? How do you ever figure out if you are part of anything? Who tells you if you fit into the world? Only you, dear friends, only you can decide for yourself if you have any importance in the grand world you live in.

So often we hear your pleas of, "Who am I? Where am I going? How do I fit in? I'm not worthy of even a name." Dear ones, we wish to tell you that you look outside of yourself for all of those answers. You depend on others, anyone to tell you of your importance. How could you ever get an honest answer from anyone if they don't feel important to themselves?

Look within, discover who you are. But in doing so do not allow that discovery to take in any words from outside of you. When one does not feel proud of their achievements it is because they are looking for external validation. Would you be surprised if I told you achievements come from within, not from without? We marvel at the power of a piece of paper. This piece of paper can say you have done this, you have achieved that and you can now achieve and be someone in your world. We do not wish to deny the value of learning from books or from your schools that have created this paper, for they are worthy. However, you are so much more than a piece of paper. That is what we would like to get across today.

If children were taught from the beginning grades about the importance of what's inside of them compared to what they can learn outside of them, your world would be a changed place. When you understand the beauty, strength and power you have inside of you and add outside learning, it is a truer picture of who you are. This is a far better achievement than the huge push to acquire what you call "credentials."

We do see a shift, a change of trying to teach these small ones who they are. But it is being marred by so much outside activity that it is being lost in the shuffle. How is it possible to create a good environment for children to learn about themselves when so much is going on in your world? We believe a shift will happen when the children are introduced to nature and the wonder of earth rather than what the manufacturing or toy companies create. Then a child's entertainment would come from within.

In the very active world you find yourself in, time is most limited. Children seem to be entertained by so much outside of them. We believe as your world becomes so bogged down with so much you will get to a point where you will all yell, "Enough!" We hope small ones will start to emerge and become leaders in your world, leaders of self. This change is happening slowly, it is hard to be different. It is difficult for both parents and children to not buy into everything that's available.

It will take a few brave young adults to start this shift, but it will happen. In many, many years to come we see plastic toys falling by the wayside. Then the adult can emerge from the child and know that no form of entertainment is necessary except self.

Carole

To understand most of this chapter in my early adult years would have been difficult. I thought the real me was who I am on the outside, in other words, my body. I certainly knew that any outside or extended schooling would add to my brainpower but I also thought that it would enhance my overall outside package in some way. I often wanted to be credentialed in some manner but realized I didn't have enough driving interest to continue on with the schooling to make it occur.

There has always been a constant chatter going on inside of me, which I dismissed as normal for a good portion of my adult years. The noise I hear is similar to a radio with a low enough volume that it is not bothersome, but rather a comforting background murmur. As I address it the sound increases. Even with this dialogue going on I did not make the connection then that the inside was really the key to who I was. Worry about how my outside appeared to others and if they thought I was good enough to earn a position in the world was my main focus.

When I switched my thinking around and realized that who I actually am was internal, my life started to blossom. Now after many years of discontent about the short length of my extended schooling, I no longer wish to achieve letters of merit after my name. As it turned out the joy work that I chose to do could be disrupted by any conflicting book knowledge, if I would let it. For my path, I must go strictly with my heart for the answers and not rely on something stored in my head that may have been learned from books or schooling. For many this extended schooling is the perfect way and a huge necessity to achieve their goals. I applaud them and all their hard work, but for me this desire has vanished and with it came a new freedom. I realize there is no degree available for the intuitive!

If we could restructure our schools by shifting the focus from outside to inside learning, I think a child's personal path would become apparent to them at a much earlier age. This might help avert the staggering high school drop out rate and help clear their thoughts of confusion about who they are, before they are carried out into the world.

"Hell is only an illusion of the human mind."
Rachelle

CHAPTER 30

Righting Yourself is Your Savior

Rachelle

Who do you look at to make everything okay? Who is famous enough to give you security? What name comes to mind to give you truth? We would like to tell you, that only you can do this. Your truth never comes from outside of you.

Your truth is not written in any book. We observe so many of you referring to certain scriptures as your way of life. How could a book such as the Bible steer you to your path? Is that because someone with such a famous name as Jesus told you this is the way in saying, "Follow me"?

If we were to look deeply into the words "Follow me," what do you think is really meant here? Jesus set himself up as an example of a way to live your life. He said that you are not any different than him; actually he said you are the same. In that interpretation does it mean that you must follow the same path he did? The Bible offers many, many ways to lead your life and be saved. But saved from what we ask, from you or from something on my side? If you do not comply is there something terrible and devious here that engulfs you into what many call hell?

Too many of his words in the scriptures have been rather misinterpreted. We see many on earth create much worse experiences for themselves than hell represents in their mind. We will tell you there is no hell here. Hell is only an illusion in the human mind. There is nothing at all even close to what the word "hell" represents to you. Here there is only togetherness, love and a knowing that we all are the same yet individuals.

If you were where I am, a peaceful energy would enfold you letting you know just how deeply loved you are. Here judgment is nonexistent. We all understand that judgment is a word from earth. For us to ever apply that word here would make no sense at all. We understand that we are all connected and to judge one would be to judge all. Total understanding of any situation that has happened on earth is also known here.

Earth is a very small portion of who you are. Do not allow a book such as the Bible to control you or to tell you who you are. We observe a book, such as that one, allows more judgment to become apparent, not less. This is not at all what Jesus was trying to teach. In a way, it has almost backfired. You might consider putting this golden book down. See if you could look within for your answers about who you are and what kind of person you are. The Bible was not intended for judgment of you at all. However, many interpretations have turned it into a book of judgments.

We observe you today in perfection. It would be most advantageous to look within and listen very carefully for your answers. Here you will find who you are, where your beauty is, and more. When you look within, listen deeply so that not one thing from outside of you can deter you from the wonderful feeling of yourself. Please don't allow anything to dictate the do's and don'ts of your life. Every one of your answers comes from within your heart. That is the true you.

If you have a negative thought about yourself just know that we will never put you into judgment, only you can do that. Punishment for being who you are can only come from yourself. Be so kind to yourself, you only have you. From our observation you are all so beautiful no matter what anyone or anything says to the contrary.

Carole

Often I could not decide which fork in the road to take, so following others was the only way for me to be assured I was going forward. Upon observing others I would follow their lead if it seemed somewhat interesting and okay to me. My opinions never seemed quite as concrete or as important as others, so I relied on their choices and direction. In this way, however, I quickly lost sight of my own likes and dislikes.

Because I was such a follower I probably would have embraced the Bible as my leader, if I had been drawn to read it. I recall that I thought hell, devils and other dark forces were in the Bible from what I had heard at my Catholic schools and I had already made my mind up that they did not exist. Rachelle says that the Bible turned into a book of judgments, even though that was not the intention. It is sad to me that it took that twist. I have a hard time trying to align a holy book with any judgment at all. In my mind the two just do not fit together. However, I do understand and honor that the Bible is a pathway for many. Although for me I must obtain my answers from within to feel secure in who I am.

"When you do not hold a respect for the elderly, you do not hold respect for yourself upon traveling in that direction.
Rachelle

CHAPTER 31

Caution in Body is Necessary for Life

Rachelle

We want to address the contribution your body gives to you. We recognize that bodies hold the highest card. It would be easy to say to you, "Bodies don't matter, souls matter." However, we know that on earth bodies do get the most attention, even higher than the development of the brain.

We recognize so many of you wish to look like a select few. Earth has set up certain models as guidelines as to what form your body should take. Many believe that the youthful look is the way to go. We see ones in their seventies or eighties still looking quite young. They may have taken thirty years off their age in looks. We are only talking about their surface appearance. Why is this so important?

Earth's biggest industry is in the line of change for the body, hair and wrinkles. What are you trying to erase? Past unhappy times, past deeds, past mistakes? Why must the skin look smooth and taut? What does that say to the onlooker? That you are fresh on earth, with fresh new ideas? Does this help you fit in with the younger generation?

Where the contradiction comes in is if you are altering yourself for others or to look like someone else. The only sadness here is when you choose to transform your look away from who you really are. Are you hiding from whom you chose to be? Would you be doing this to escape yourself? Or would you just be doing this as a form of maintenance, to feel and look fresher for yourself? There are not any models that are more correct than others for ways to look. It is only the running away from self that seems a concern. As your brow becomes droopy would it be possible to bless that part of you for the many years of experience you have under your belt? In no way are we saying that you do not have a right to do whatever you choose with yourself. Please give yourself permission to alter in any way. For us, you are accepted by any choice you make.

People will not be striving to look different when the older generation is respected for who they are, for their accomplishments and what they can still achieve. When you do not hold a respect for the elderly, you do not hold respect for yourself upon traveling in that direction. Your bodies will be cast away when you no longer need them. As you experience the shedding you will realize the amount of energy that was put into changing the shell into who you think you should have looked like. In fact, what you are actually left with is who you really are. If you choose to direct your energy to develop the parts of who you are, the disappointment you feel upon leaving your body would be minimal. Try to understand the all of you. The whole of you will not be damaged in any way by these constant changes you put upon self.

Bodies come in many shapes and sizes; is one better than another? What is your ideal? Try not to tamper with the reality of the size you chose. You would have an uphill battle all the way to try to transform your body type into one that now looks more appealing to you. Be grateful and gracious in your choice. You are perfect in looks; you are perfect in size for this very moment of who you are.

You mean so much to us and we love who you represent to us. Please take this to heart and be you.

Carole

My days of longing to look like others have long passed, but I was not prepared for the wrinkles that came along with aging. Those were always reserved for old people or someone else. I certainly thought wrinkles would elude me somehow.

When I was young the thought of reaching twenty-one was appealing. To be called an adult was enticing, but that longing soon passed as I found the years continued to come in rapid secession. Wrinkles began appearing with little warning. In the beginning my changing skin was quite a concern for me and I did everything to avert it. With all the technology now, aging and wrinkles for the face and most of the body could be obsolete, even for the elderly.

For my own sanity I have decided to let my body age as it wishes, with only a little maintenance on my part. To keep up with all that is available on the market and through the medical field is more external focus than I now want to be concerned with.

Rachelle seems to offer the key in this chapter to accepting our aging bodies. If we were to have a deep respect for the elderly, like some cultures do, we may choose to wear our wrinkles as a badge of honor and not try to erase them.

"Children come with a desire to be who they are."
Rachelle

CHAPTER 32

Your Heart is Your Source of Trust

Rachelle

Upon observation we notice our lovely friends on earth most often choose to be led to places other than where their heart is directing. We find heads have accumulated so much data as to what is proper and what is not. Would it surprise you if most, or even all, of this data is not yours? We also notice earth certainly likes to take polls. These can often create excitement that is part of the drama and a part of the swaying.

From infancy on you start to fill your brain with so much of others' past experiences. You rely on this information heavily for your do's and don'ts. We must ask how could anyone in any circumstance be exactly the same as you?

We see many of you holding up your hands in despair saying, "What should we do with these naughty children?" Where has respect gone, respect for others, and for themselves? How did this world become so violent? It appears to us there are a lot of very bright and confused children who are saying, "I will think for myself." They feel they are powerful in doing this; rules are not for them. The truth is rules should apply to no one.

We believe there would be no violence if each one could be responsible for themselves without having to connect with a data bank of do's and don'ts. You were not born violent. How do ones become this way? What are they challenging? Perhaps it's as simple as challenging other people's ways, ways they may object about how they must conform in order to live on earth.

Think of your small child, eight or nine years of age—do you give them reflections of your past, listing all your do's and don'ts? Are you passing on all your fears to your child? Why must you give such heavy warnings to your little ones? In doing this, are you saying to them that they are not capable of surviving without all these fears? Is it possible these children, who become so angry, are tired of being pushed and shoved into someone else's ideal?

When can you let go? When can you start giving your children credit for who they are? Is it when they are nine, twelve or must they be eighteen or twenty-one years old in order to be called an adult? We observe a crippling effect is put upon the child when they feel they must conform for the sake of someone else's view. Ones who possess so much anger are not bad children. When you can teach them to be who they are, and you back that up one hundred percent, they will be able to stand in their own convictions. The taunting and teasing will then have no effect on them. An expanded awareness is being felt as these young ones come to earth.

Children come with a desire to be who they are. Can you allow this without fear? To accomplish this you must learn as adults to be okay with yourselves. How many of you right now are affected in any way by what others think? If you are affected, do you conform to what is proper by earth's standards?

Could you take a deeper look at what comes over the airways, computers and movie screens and realize that movie heroes often tend to act violently and look different. This is all fine and well but the problem arises when children believe this is correct, and think that the only way to survive is to have violence as their shield. They also feel the need to be armed in case of intruders.

We are most pleased to see a shift with the change to a new and softer awareness of who you are. But at this moment it seems to be so overshadowed by the violence.

Are these children only stating, "Here I am, love me for who I am?" They feel a need to protect their freedom to be themselves, and feel that no one understands them. If adults could drop their judgment, the children would drop their defenses. Then you, dear ones, would be living in a world filled with peace.

Carole

When Rachelle stated that our heads are filled with others' data she again confirmed for me that any knowledge from that source really has nothing to do with us, or our path. And if the rest of the stored information is from our past experiences then our heads really are not a very reliable source for our current or future guidance.

For several years I have tried diligently to live by my heart. It has led me to explore different avenues that I feel I would not have thought of before. I have taken risks that wanted to be vetoed by my head, only to find out that the end result created an opening for something else I was seeking. I noticed that the heart knows the perfect conclusion will happen, where as the head often wishes to be in fear and stop the idea from beginning.

My heart knowledge certainly can conflict with my head. Sometimes I feel almost alone with my inner beliefs, but the strength of its truth is undeniable for me. Even though I often feel like a fish trying to swim up stream with my unconventional reality, I know there are many more people like myself who trust their hearts for their guidance.

Our youngest child has recently turned twenty-one; which deems him to be an adult. But when I see him moving out of state and stepping out into the world alone I am reminded how young and vulnerable I was at that age. As his mother, my old ways might wish to caution him with my own and others' past experiences to better prepare him for what is ahead. However, Rachelle has spoken such wisdom about our younger generation that I have absorbed her advice. What she says feels so right! For me to assume that I know what is better than any of my children do for their own life path is absurd. My old fears certainly do not have to become theirs. My love for them does not have to extend into warnings for their safety. I hold a respect for their own inner guidance and ways to their path.

It would be exciting to see positive changes our world could take if we would all allow even our very young children a little slack and encourage them to think for themselves without our dated input.

*"We are here in the wings, waiting for any hint from you that you
would invite guidance."*
Rachelle

CHAPTER 33

We Conclude With Love

Many questions have been asked. We hope we have been able to
comply with the answers you are seeking.

So much is happening and changing at an accelerated speed in
your world. Do not let this alarm you. Do you ever have a desire to
turn the clock back to slow things down, as it was a century ago?
Would it be possible that the engines on earth have been revved to
such a high speed that it might be time for an idle to reflect on what
has been achieved, and accomplished on earth? Where has the last
hundred years gone? Does the world look anything today like it did
back then? What have you learned? What has survived? What has
not survived? Upon observation of your questions, wants, desires,
and longings, it is our belief that many of you are looking for a slower
paced life. Perhaps looking back into some areas that appeal to you
might offer some of your answers. Have people taken a back seat to
electronics and computerization? Are you now a number, a person
with no face?

Children today are your hope for the brightest future. The turmoil
you have witnessed on the earth, both in human violence and
destruction by extreme weather, is really a crying out to stop, stop
and reflect why you chose to be on your great planet at this time.

We love each one of you, we see no difference whatsoever in the
quality from one person to another. Each one of you have sufficient
strength to be who you are, to step off an illusionary treadmill and
say to yourself, "Who am I? Why am I here? Is what I am doing each

day of any importance to who I am?" Each one of you has the strength to know you are a spiritual being. Earth is only there for a mere visit by you. Discover your spiritual roots, put down your hostility, your guard and put down your fears. When ones on earth can stop all judgment of themselves and others, it would be possible to do all those things I just mentioned.

Many on earth feel they must protect and arm themselves from others. In doing this are you really arming yourself from who you think you are? We will tell you who you really are; you are love, wholeness and completeness. You must know that what we see is the truth. You must realize that no one on earth is any more complete than you are. I am speaking from your home. Earth can also feel the same way. Could you think of earth as a wonderful vacation, a place to learn, to explore and to find out who you are?

Please remember we are only an arm's length away, and are here to guide you. To us you are wonderful, we hold no judgment; only you can put that upon yourself. We are here in the wings, waiting for any hint from you that you would invite any guidance. We do not profess to be any smarter than you are, it's only that we do not have a narrowed vision; we can see the larger picture. You have been just like us numerous times. We have only changed positions for now; you have helped in guiding us before and now, if asked, we will help you.

So many of us surround earth, constantly waiting for your beck and call. We come to you in a way of feeling, feeling what's right for you. Please know you are never alone and you are always loved.

Thank you.
Rachelle

Carole

Rachelle has surely offered us many ideas and insights for a more loving and peaceful world. It all sounds so simple, but so much of our thinking and doing would have to be practically reversed to our present ways.

It is my belief that in time we can achieve peace for our planet and ourselves. This may come faster if we would not wait for others and the world around us to change, but instead could look within ourselves for this transformation. Each of us within our own families might be able to take baby steps towards adopting a new view or change offered by Rachelle. As we change this new view and awareness would travel easily outside our families, thus creating a domino effect of change for our world. It is, of course, our choice. I love to envision the positive changes that could come within all of our families by incorporating the expanded awareness of Rachelle's words. I cannot think of a better gift of love than that for ourselves, our families, and in turn the outside world.

The making of this book has spanned over eight years. I have watched while thirty-two seasons have started and completed their eye pleasing cycles in our beautiful Northwest. Change has become evident. As I reflect back to the beginning of this journey I find little in common with the younger Carole who contributed in the early chapters. The shy, timid, questioning, very cautious woman on a search for self of yesteryear has slowly evaporated as each chapter of this book has unfolded its enlightened awareness through Cameron and Rachelle's words. They offered me a desired life through their broadened spirit wisdom, but I had no idea that my acceptance would expand to make it this enticingly beautiful! I offer them my unconditional love and deep gratitude.

"When you call, we all come."
Rachelle

Cheryl

Finished. The word rolls in my mind pleasingly as I savor the completion of this book, yet I realize it begins a new life. Now it goes forth to you. That is the reason it was given, shared, written and published.

I have watched the growth in my life and Carole's from this inner and outer journey we have made; as we listened, absorbed, questioned ourselves and lived the many insights shared by Cameron and Rachelle in this book.

We have all asked the questions they came to answer at one time or another. We observed that Cameron and Rachelle's answers are not glib or dictatorial, quite the opposite. They share their knowledge and also ask us to think, by their questions to us on a variety of subjects. I believe we do know the answers to their questions if we listen to the wisdom within each of us. The problem seems to be that with our busy lives we do not take the time to go within and actually listen. It is easier to take someone else's opinion or stay with what we have always done.

I know what busy is, as you do too. However, I have found that it does not take a large chunk of time, sometimes only seconds or a minute to check in, to feel and know through our heart-soul. How often my mind conflicts with that wisdom within. But time and again I weigh the two and when I go with the wisdom within, life flows.

Cameron's foundational wisdom and the tools he shares are invaluable. They are the keys to unlock the doors of our minds to new concepts and ways of living fully with more awareness than before. Rachelle opened another door into a vaster universe and a living earth that I had only partly glimpsed before. Because Carole and I listened and absorbed their wisdom our lives opened up, new insights occurred to us about both everyday things and how we view our world.

For instance, I have always been startled and a bit afraid of lizards. So is it any surprise that my husband and I have cabin in the Southern Oregon woods that seems to be the primary territory for these creatures? I found them everywhere, in the cabin, hanging on the large oak tree outside, on the deck, on my walks and I jumped every time I saw one. One dry, hot summer day I saw a lizard on the oak tree at my eye level. He was basking in the sun next to dried moss clinging to the bark. This time, however, I remembered that we are all connected, yes, even to lizards. So I filled a glass with water and held it above the moss and lizard. His eyes watched me carefully but he held his ground. Slowly I poured a small stream down the bark and moss. As it came next to him his eyes darted to the water then back at me. This repeated. Then he began to drink the water. Finishing, he looked back at me and in that instant we connected! He understood my peace offering. I have not been frightened of lizards since, in fact I feel that connection every time I see one.

Breaking through our barriers of fear and separation, recognizing the absolute unity of life in our world is the essence of what is shared in this book. We change our world, personally and collectively, as we expand our understanding and challenge old fears and limiting concepts. It is drawing a circle big enough in our minds to encompass everything; all people, all creatures; all that is. That takes change within; for every one of us has some area of our life that is outside our comfort zones. Sometimes it takes courage, and not following the crowd, to make a change. Carole and I have found this is where we want to be, where freedom exists, barriers melt and life blends with Love. We will meet you there.

Epilogue

The grand design for each of us seems to have a way of unfolding even when we're not looking. Near the completion of this manuscript I received the news that my mother had made a very peaceful transition to the other side. I am humbled that she chose to pass over so quietly, without illness as an aid. My concern with the release of this book was that my words in Part 1 could add to the burden my mother already seemed to be carrying. This has now been erased.

Mother is now free. Her bondage to earth has vanished. The play is done; the curtains are drawn, every scene chosen by my parents to act out in this life are over. Many scenes were so difficult. They performed their parts so well that in time I was able to become strong, seek my path and most importantly be who I really am. Bless them for that.

I have moved through many long stages of disbelief; fear, betrayal, and more to attain my present knowing and feeling of unconditional love for my parents. For us to be able to connect now, while they are in their spirit state, is a gift of immense comfort for me. May their souls rejoice, for they are truly home.

Love, Carole